# Table of Contents

# Introduction

This is a three part study of what was almost certainly, for the short period of time that it lasted, the world's greatest revival—The Welsh Revival. There is no other example in either Biblical or church history in which a region was so quickly or radically transformed for righteousness, or the world so impacted, as happened during this revival. The fire of this move of God was so intense that when letters or newspaper stories about the revival were read in other parts of the world, revival would break out there. Today, almost a century after it happened, those who just read or hear the story are still impacted with both profound conviction, and hope.

The inevitable question for us is: Will God do it again? Yes! That is the purpose of this study. It is exciting and inspiring to hear about the great things that God has done, but the purpose for the excitement and inspiration is so that He can do it again—with us. The Scriptures declare that the greatest move of God of all time will occur at the end of this age. The Welsh Revival, as great as it was, was but a foretaste of something much greater that is coming.

One of the most important questions that any believer, church or ministry can ask today is how to get ready for the great harvest that is the end of this age. With the exception of the advents of Christ, this harvest will unquestionably be the greatest event in the history of the world. The greatest proportion of Bible prophecy focuses on this period, and the significant events in church history are in preparation for it. The church is not here to be an observer—we are here to light the world on fire! The fire that is about to be lit will burn until every bit of wood, hay, and stubble is consumed—and the gold, silver and precious stones are purified.

There are prophetic parallels found in the history of the Welsh Revival that can help to guide us in the necessary preparation for these times. The church in Wales, and the community of Wales, were remarkable parallels of the church today, and the condition of society. We can see in this history an accurate map that can show us where we have been, where we are now, and where we are going.

Understanding how the spiritual foundation was laid for this great revival can help us to understand the foundation that the Lord is today laying in His church to prepare for the harvest. Understanding what was done correctly can help us to do the right things. Likewise, honestly looking at the mistakes can help us to avoid making the same ones—as a wise man once stated: "Those who do not know history are doomed to repeat it."

There are many aspects of this great revival that we want to repeat, and there are many that we want to avoid. The foundation of the contemporary church contains potential for both the coming revival and the similar catastrophic mistakes. It seems that the great interest that is now being stirred in the church to study history is the grace of God to help us to do it right this time. Let us not neglect so great a grace.

# PART I

# A Foundation
# For Revival

# Chapter One

# The Fire Begins

In 1904 one of the greatest revivals in history broke out in Wales, a small principality of the British Isles. There have been a few spiritual awakenings in history to span the globe and touch millions, but it can be argued that none had as much concentrated power and impact as the Welsh Revival. It seems that the Lord looked down upon Wales and said, "I am going to show the church and the world what I can do with just a handful of faithful saints who will yield themselves to Me." The results of that demonstration still send shock waves of conviction and hope to all who hear the story.

Evan Roberts was the most popular evangelist of the Welsh Revival. He is also one of the more enigmatic figures in church history. Roberts was not a dynamic leader of people. He did not come with new doctrines, nor was he even considered a good preacher. He came as a great example of a dynamic *follower* of the Lord, encouraging the church to be a proper host to the Holy Spirit. As both the Scriptures and history testify, the more yielded that we are to the Holy Spirit, the more He will use us. Evan Roberts must be considered one of the greatest examples of a vessel yielded to the Holy Spirit.

As the news of the Welsh Revival spread around the world, some of the great preachers and spiritual leaders of the time came to witness it. Some called it a "Pentecost greater than Pentecost." Many of these leaders came thinking that they could give direction and leadership to this new movement. There was a concern that such a great revival was being run by teenagers and even children. Evan Roberts was only in his mid-twenties and most of the evangelists and workers in the revival were in fact teenagers and children. But when these great and renowned preachers arrived in Wales, they were so impacted by the presence of the Holy Spirit that they sat dumb and mute before Him and the children He had chosen. In the presence of this revival it was quickly understood that the Lord Himself was in control, and that He alone would choose whom He would use for His work.

When the glory of the Lord fills His temple all flesh and presumption flees! This was to be a hallmark of the Welsh Revival. Great knowledge and eloquence bowed the knee to love and pure devotion just as the "unlearned and un-trained" apostles had stood before the Sanhedrin in Jerusalem. One of the great preachers of that era, G. Campbell Morgan, testified that he would trade all of his learning for even a portion of the presence of God that accompanied these children. This was the common response as great pulpiteering, or the great leadership ability to mobilize people for projects, seemed pale and insignificant in the presence of the anointing.

## Grace Comes To The Humble

There is a great difference between preaching from a source of knowledge and preaching from a well of living water that flows from the throne of God. This was to be one of the central lessons of the Welsh Revival. When God decides that He is going to move, He does not look for those wise enough or educated enough—He looks for those who are yielded and humble enough to risk following Him. In

Wales the Lord demonstrated that when He finds such vessels there is no limit to what He can do through them.

While the revival spread into almost every nook and corner of the country, the ministry of Evan Roberts was mostly confined to just one of its twelve counties. The fire of God burned in towns and villages which he did not visit. In many of the places which he did visit, he found the fire was already there. He would fan the flame a little and then go back to his base. Even Roberts knew from the beginning that he was neither the source nor the perpetuator of what was happening. He simply tried to stay yielded to the Spirit so that he could play whatever part was required of him.

That the Lord has chosen men to be His habitation must be one of the great marvels of the creation. But God has also chosen men to *do* His work, and He often uses just a single individual to ignite a new move of His Holy Spirit. We see this in Scripture with such men as Peter, Paul, or John the Baptist. There are many historical examples such as Hus, Luther, Calvin, Knox, Zinzendorf, Wesley, Edwards, Finney or Seymore, who were used to ignite great spiritual advances. However, even though the Lord does often use a single individual to ignite the fires of revival or to lead a spiritual advance, there have always been others prepared to keep the fires going and to lay a proper foundation for the gains that are made. The same was true in the Welsh Revival. Evan Roberts undoubtedly struck the match, but there were many who carried the flames, and many others who had prepared the timber for the fires. Few of these ever became well known with men, but they are certainly bright stars in the eternal chronicles of the Book of Life.

Few men in history have been able to differentiate between being used by God and trying to use God. A Christian teacher once defined *profanity* as "the seeking of one's own recognition at the expense of God's glory." Evan Roberts was driven by that conviction. He was utterly jealous to see that only the Lord received the glory. For as long as Evan maintained that devotion, and as long as he imparted it to the workers, the fires of revival did not go out. From the beginning until the end, this was one revival that could not be attributed to human charisma or promotional ability.

## You Do Not Have To Advertise A Fire

A true move of God is not fueled by money, organization or advertising. True revival only comes when the pillar of fire, that is the presence of God Himself, picks up and moves. To try to organize, promote or sell a move of God is profanity in its lowest form. Historians would later write that the most astonishing feature of the Welsh Revival was the lack of commercialism. There were no hymn books, no song leaders, no committees, no choirs, no great preachers, no offerings, no organization. Yet souls were redeemed, families were healed and whole cities were converted on a scale that had not been seen before or since.

James Stewart, a historian of the Welsh Revival, researched the newspapers and magazines published in Wales in 1904 and 1905 and could not find a single advertisement promoting meetings. The only organized or planned evangelistic campaign for Evan Roberts was a single meeting in Liverpool in 1905. But even in that meeting the Lord disrupted the plans and radically changed the agenda before the evangelist arrived.

# Chapter Two

# The Plan Was Not To Plan

Broken plans seemed to be the hallmark of the Welsh Revival. Just weeks before it broke out in his home church in Loughor, Evan had planned campaigns throughout Wales with his brother Dan and a friend named Sydney Evans. Quickly he discovered that the Spirit had another plan, and His plans were much better. Evan soon developed a healthy fear of man's planning and organization in the midst of revival.

This is not to imply that leadership and organization are not at times needed in the church, but when the Spirit is doing something new and fresh, the greatest gift is not knowing how to lead, but knowing how to follow. The attempts at organization during the Welsh Revival all proved futile, and at times a hindrance to the true work. It seems that every time the Spirit wants to move in a creative way He still has to find those who are "formless and void." Those with the humility that comes from knowing they do not have the answers, which stimulates a holy desperation

**15**

for God in them, seem to be the only ones who can ever be responsive to the Lord when He wants to do a new thing.

Evan Roberts refused to allow his meetings or visits to a city to be announced until a day or two before he was to arrive. Even then he would only say that he "hoped" to be at a certain place at a certain time. As the Lord Jesus explained to Nicodemus: **"The wind blows where it wishes and you hear the sound of it, but do not know where it comes from and where it is going; so is everyone who is born of the Spirit"** (John 3:8). The workers in the Welsh Revival came to understand that the Lord meant this literally. Finally they did not try to figure out where the Spirit was going next, they only tried to stay close enough to "hear the sound of it." The workers came to abhor the presumption that the Spirit would automatically go with them and bless their own plans. They knew that the Spirit did not follow them, but that they must follow the Spirit.

It is noteworthy that many who have tried to duplicate this kind of ministry style succumbed to spiritual delusions or have even suffered the shipwreck of their faith. Even the apostles to the early church often planned their missionary journeys and would announce months ahead of time their impending visits. Yet, they always remained open for the Lord to change their plans; nevertheless, the apostles could not always keep their intentions to visit a city, as with Paul's attempts to revisit the Corinthians.

The point is that our renewed minds are not in conflict with the Holy Spirit. The Lord did not lead the apostles around by the hand, He *sent* them. They made many of their own decisions because they had His mind. But because they were always growing and maturing they did not always make the right decisions. At times the Lord would correct their course with an intervention of divine guidance through a dream, vision, or a prophet. We must labor with the spiritual wisdom that has been given to us, but always be open for the Lord to intervene and change our plans.

During times of a dynamic outpouring of the Holy Spirit, such as the Welsh Revival, the Lord can only use those who will yield themselves completely to Him in order that He might do something entirely new. It seems that in every city the apostle Paul visited, the Holy Spirit moved differently than in the previous ones. Paul moved with vision, strategy and decisiveness, but with a finely tuned sensitivity to the Holy Spirit, and the willingness to yield to a different plan.

Many of the great missionary ventures in church history, such as William Booth's Salvation Army, were planned over many years, and they generally followed the plan. Those who might have worked with some of these missionary ventures would probably scorn the lack of organization of the Welsh Revival. Likewise, those who were a part of the Welsh Revival would almost certainly reject the seeming over-dependence on organization that such missionary societies had. A great tribute to General Booth was that he visited the Welsh Revival, observed that it was functioning in almost the opposite manner in which he ran the Salvation Army, and was still able to recognize that it was God and should not be tampered with. He then went back and continued to run the army just the way he had been, recognizing that God employs *different* strategies for different places or purposes.

We must realize that the God who makes every snowflake different seldom moves the same way twice. It is His nature to be creative and diverse. There are lessons for the whole church in the way the Lord moved in Wales. Likewise, there are lessons for us all in the way that He moved through the Salvation Army in its early years. The Welsh Revival actually died because it took the fear of organization and fear of human intervention too far. Likewise, the Salvation Army, though still a large organization and doing many good works, is spiritually only a shell of its former glory because the organization was not flexible enough to hold new wine.

## Seek The Wine, Not The Wineskin

Those who have tried to duplicate the original glory of the Salvation Army have, for the most part, failed. Those who have tried to duplicate the Welsh Revival have often become pitiful caricatures of the original revivalists. There does not seem to be a single example in church history where a wineskin of church organization was built before the new wine of revival was given. This does not necessarily mean that it cannot be done, just that it has not yet been done, and does seem to be most improbable. Those who have tried to build the wineskin first have often found themselves out of step and unable to receive the new wine when it came. The Lord has never restricted Himself to move by any predetermined formula. There is one quality common to those who have been mightily used by the Holy Spirit—they were able to hear the sound of the Holy Spirit moving and were willing to move the way that He wanted to for that time and place.

The lessons of this great revival are critically important for the last day church to understand because she will see the greatest harvest of all. As the Lord Jesus testified: *"THE HARVEST is the end of the age"* (Matthew 13:39). The important lessons of the Welsh Revival must be combined with the knowledge of many different ways that the Lord has chosen to move in other places and at other times, if they are to be properly understood. All of this knowledge must be received with the humility to comprehend that we cannot know or understand all that can be known or understood about the way God moves. We must remain open for Him to act in ways that we do not understand or have not heard of before.

Evan Roberts greatly feared man's planning and organization and that made him a fit vessel for what the Lord wanted to do in Wales in 1904. When the campaign was finally organized for his visit to Liverpool, it was a good example of Evan's uncompromising commitment to walk in the way that he understood. The committee pressed him to state a definite time when he would come. He refused to do it. When he did eventually go he gave the committee only four days warning that he was coming. Even then, though 100,000 Welsh people in that English city were longing and waiting to hear him, he insisted that he could not know in which of the crowded chapels he would speak at a given time.

Dan Roberts and Sydney Evans had just turned twenty when the revival broke out but they were used to reap a mighty harvest. They followed the same procedure as Evan. They sought the Lord daily for His will and they went where He told them to go. They knew that apart from the presence and power of the Holy Spirit they would accomplish nothing. When they arrived in a place, sometimes they preached and sometimes they did not. Sometimes they kept silent during the entire services which often lasted for four or five hours.

# Chapter Three

# No Superstars

During the Welsh Revival people came to the meetings for God, not a superstar. They crowded chapels to overflowing, not even knowing whether an evangelist would be there or not. Sometimes Evan Roberts would enter a meeting and sit on the front seat and say nothing for three hours. Then he would stand up, preach and pray for some ten or fifteen minutes and sit down. Sometimes he might preach the whole time, or pray the whole time. Sometimes he would sit silently through the entire meeting. Regardless of what Evan did, the people would carry on under the influence of the Holy Spirit.

There were soloists, duos and special singers during the revival, but they seldom announced where they were going to sing. Sometimes they went to a place expecting to sing, but the Spirit had other plans and they would keep their peace, or they might just pray. Those who witnessed their ministry only had the witness that when they did sing it *was* the Holy Spirit. This was a revival in which the Lord Jesus Christ, Himself, was the center and the main attraction. "It was noised abroad that HE was in the house." The young workers knew that the Holy Spirit came to testify of Jesus and if an evangelist or the evangelistic party became the center of the attraction, then the Holy Spirit would depart.

Evan Roberts knew that he was popular and he dreaded publicity, because he felt that it detracted from the One who was the true Source of the Revival. He dreaded newspaper reporters. He dreaded adulation. Many times he withdrew himself from the meetings when he felt that the people were coming to see and hear him instead of coming for the Lord. In meetings where he felt that he was the center of attraction he pleaded with an agonized spirit that the people would look away to Christ and Him alone, or else the Holy Spirit would withdraw Himself from them. Though Evan Roberts became the most publicized preacher in the world at that time, he repeatedly refused interviews with reporters, who came from every part of the globe. He refused to be photographed except by members of his own family. He knew this awakening was of God and not from himself and that if people idolized him the Glory would be withdrawn. He did not even answer the multitude of requests that came from publishing houses around the world seeking to write his biography. He greatly feared that by doing this he might rob the Lord of even some of the glory that was due only to Him.

## To Speak Or Not To Speak

"Being led by the Spirit requires knowing when not to speak as much as when to speak." Evan Roberts was a wonderful demonstration of this sensitivity to the Lord. During a meeting he would often sit among the people without saying a word. Visitors from different parts of the world were astonished as they observed him letting the course of crowded gatherings be dictated entirely by the people's sensitivity to the Spirit as they sang, prayed, and testified. F.B. Meyer, a mature and renowned Christian leader, upon watching him in the meetings, explained, "He will not go in front of the divine Spirit, but is willing to stand aside and remain in the background unless he is perfectly sure that the Spirit of God is moving him." Then he added, "It is a profound lesson for us all!". The one who knows when not to speak will speak with more authority when he does speak.

Christian leaders who had come from the ends of the earth stood in awe and bowed in adoration to God as they witnessed the revival. General William Booth, Gypsy Rodney Smith, F.B. Meyer, G. Campbell Morgan and many other renowned men of God came to marvel at this great visitation. In most cases they only prayed or said a few words. Sometimes they sat quietly in the meetings while young people, and even children prayed, sang, and testified in the Spirit. The men of God who came all quickly recognized that this was not a revival that came through great preachers or great preaching; this was a supernatural work altogether apart from either. To their credit, most of these men quickly understood that their very personalities would actually hinder the meetings and they yielded to the Holy Spirit. Great preaching is loved by all who love the Word of God, but these great preachers all knew that their great preaching had never produced the kind of Presence of the Lord they encountered in Wales.

## The Children Enter The Kingdom

We are seeing in this decade of the nineteen nineties a great movement to equip and train the children and youth in the ways of the Lord, to help them become fruitful members of the Body of Christ. This movement is of the Lord and it is significant, but the Welsh Revival was quite different. In Wales it was the children and youth who sought to equip their parents and train the adults in the ways of the Lord. The Lord said that we had to become like little children to enter the kingdom—they may have more to teach us than we have to teach them!

Evan Roberts was only twenty-six years of age when the revival broke out. His sister, Mary who was such an important part of the work, was sixteen. Their brother Dan and Mary's future husband, Sydney Evans, were both about twenty. The "Singing Sisters", who were greatly used, were between the ages of eighteen and twenty-two. Thousands of young people were converted and immediately sent throughout over the land testifying to the glory of God. Little children had their own prayer meetings and witnessed boldly to even the most hardened sinners. The chapels overflowed with the young.

## A New Song   (The new song)

Spontaneous worship that gives birth to a new form of worship is usually found in true revivals. This was also true of the Welsh Revival. This too probably could not have happened had there been just one strong worship leader in the meetings. There were worship leaders present, but they yielded, understanding that this revival was not for the purpose of birthing new superstars, but to glorify Jesus. This allowed the Holy Spirit to give birth to new songs and to a new form of worship that had not been previously known.

Much of the contemporary style of worship that is now attributed to either the Pentecostal or Charismatic movements actually had its origin in Wales. This revival was exploding in Wales at the same time as the Pentecostal outpouring was beginning on Azusa Street in Los Angeles. The leaders of these two revivals, Seymore and Bartleman in Los Angeles and Roberts in Wales, wrote to each other during the revivals. There was also a great deal of other interchange between the revivals as people hungry for God rushed from one to the other seeking His presence. Naturally they impacted one another. One of the great contributions of the Welsh revival was the new spontaneous form of worship called "singing in the Spirit" that was to become a signature of the Holy Spirit's presence for decades to come. R.B. Jones, a leader in the revival, said of the music:

> The fact is, unless heard, it is unimaginable and when heard indescribable. There was no hymnbook. No one gave out a hymn. Just anyone would start the singing, and very rarely did it happen that the hymn started was out of harmony with the mood at the

moment. Once started, as if moved by a simultaneous impulse, the hymn was caught up by the whole congregation almost as if what was about to be sung had been announced and all were responding to the baton of a visible human leader. I have seen nothing like it. You felt that the thousand or fifteen hundred persons before you had become merged into one myriad-headed, but simple-souled personality. Such was the perfect blending of the mood and purpose that it bore eloquent testimony to a unity created only by the Spirit of God." Another witness testified: "The praying and singing were both wonderful. There was no need for an organ. The assembly was its own organ as a thousand sorrowing or rejoicing hearts found expression in the Psalmody of their native hills.

# Chapter Four

# The Power Of Prayer

The Welsh revival was initiated and carried by a devotion to prayer and intercession that also spread throughout the worldwide Christian community. Much of the fire that continues in some of the great prayer movements of today could likely trace their origin to a lingering spark from the Welsh Revival. The prayer and the praise mingled together in most of the meetings. James E. Stewart wrote:

> It was praying that rent the heavens; praying that received direct answers there and then. The spirit of intercession was so mightily poured out that the whole congregation would take part simultaneously for hours! Strangers were startled to hear the young and unlettered pray with such unction and intelligence as they were swept up to the Throne of Grace by the Spirit of God. Worship and adoration was unbounded. Praise began to mingle with the petitions as answered prayer was demonstrated before their very eyes. Often when unsaved loved ones were the focus of the intercession, they would be compelled to come to the very meeting and be saved!

✝  This further fed the fires of both the worship and the intercession. When the believers understood that God really did hear their prayers, prayer quickly rose to the highest priority in their lives. As they prayed with more faith, they began to see quick answers to them. When they became increasingly specific in their requests, the answers became even more spectacular. They would pray for specific friends or family members in one meeting, and that person would be at the altar seeking salvation in the next one. This would fan the flames of intercession even more. This unquestionably fanned the flames of the revival.

Prayer meetings that had been drudgery before, became the main attractions, even for entire cities. Meetings swelled until overflowing, both with people and with the anointing. Meetings that were expected to be regular services, quickly became prayer meetings, as it became the first nature of everyone to pray. Groups walking to work would start praying and soon they would be joined by a swelling crowd who were drawn by the anointing. Spontaneous prayer meetings started in shops, homes and there were even cases when factories shut down so that the workers could pray. At the peak of the revival, the whole population of towns were gathering to march around their neighborhoods and claim them for Christ. On at least several occasions, the population of a town would march to a neighboring town to pray for it, and the revival would inevitably be ignited there. This revival was a witness that few things can so energize believers as when they discover the power of prayer.

## They Saved Souls

The main focus of prayer in this revival was always for the lost. There can be no revival without soul-winning, and in saving lost souls the Welsh Revival must be considered one of the most intense and effective revivals of all time. This revival was not a program for using a few preachers, or a campaign to get church members testifying to the saving grace of the Lord Jesus. There were no classes given on how to reach the lost. It just seemed like every Christian in Wales erupted simultaneously with a burning agony for the lost. The joy of salvation simply could not be contained by the believers as every coal mine, tramcar, office, school or shop became a pulpit for the gospel. Even more than the preaching, it was the witness of the common believers which led multiplied thousands to a saving faith in Jesus. There was no set pattern of strategy for the witnessing; it was simply born out of an overflowing joy and faith that could not be contained in those who knew the Savior.

The presence of the Lord was so intense in Wales that those who had travelled from the ends of the earth to witness it said that just being in one of the revival meetings was worth the whole journey—even if Evan, Dan or Sidney Roberts was not there. Methodists claimed that it was a revival of the Wesley meetings of a century before. The people of Wales lost a lot of sleep because they were afraid that if they left the services they would miss something wonderful. The meetings carried on till two and three o'clock in the morning many times, and did not end until the people, sometimes including the entire population of a city or town, had marched through the streets singing the praises of The Lamb!

It was simply impossible for an unbeliever to escape this overpowering witness, or not to be drawn into it by the sheer love and zeal of the people. Just as it is easy to identify a man or a woman who is in love, as their lover dominates their minds and conversation, Wales fell so in love with Jesus that adoration for Him lifted His name above anything else that could have captured the people's attention. The knowledge of the Lord simply washed over Wales just as the waters cover the sea. As Jesus was lifted up all men came.

## They Knew How To Carry The Ark

The Ark of the Covenant represented God's presence to the ancient nation of Israel. There are many great lessons in the Old Testament stories of the Ark concerning how we should, and should not, treat the presence of the Lord. When the Ark was treated as holy and was carried before them into battle, great and miraculous victories were won. When the Ark was not treated as holy, but was used as a good luck charm, they lost the Ark and the battle and it was captured by their enemies.

One of the greatest reasons why the Welsh Revival burned so brightly, and for so long, is that the leaders knew how to carry the "Ark" of God's presence. They knew how to remain open and submitted to the Lord's leading and how not to offend the Spirit. Those who were used so mightily in this revival were loathe to say anything that might draw attention to themselves and away from the Savior. As Psalm 25:14 states, **"The secret of the Lord is for those who fear Him,"** and they wanted to be close enough to Him to know His deepest secrets, so they learned to respect Him properly. Combined with their great love for the Lord, they had a profound and holy fear of offending Him. They loved the Ark of His presence and could not be content without having it with them, but they also reverenced it enough to learn how to handle it properly.

In this great awakening there was no ministry building, no boasting in men, but only in the Lord. When the glory of the Lord really does rest on an earthen vessel it is not the vessel that receives the attention! We must heed Peter's warning: **"Humble yourselves, therefore, under the mighty hand of God, that He may exalt you at the proper time"** (I Peter 5:6). It is our job to humble ourselves; it is God's job to exalt. If we try to do His job, He will do our job! Because the leaders of the Welsh revival were utterly committed to humbling themselves, God did exalt them. They refused to send out newsletters to build their own ministries, so the Lord used the front page of almost every major newspaper in the world to spread the word of what He was doing in Wales. As soon as He found the people humble enough to handle His promotion, He gave it to them.

We can build influence by self-promotion, but God will promote only those who do not promote themselves. That which is built on self-promotion will have to be maintained by human striving. Those who allow God to build the house have taken a yoke that is easy and a burden that is light. Those who allow God to build the work will not be worn out by the work, but will be refreshed in it.

No man can tear down that which God builds. When we are doing the work of God we do not carry the worries and fears that those who have built on self-promotion must carry. **"Everything God does will remain forever"** (Ecclesiastes 3:14). The fruit of the work that God initiates will remain. The work that is built on self-promotion inevitably ends in tragedy and disappointment. Though it is apparent that the high state of the Welsh Revival itself did not last, some of the fruit of it did. It was able to impart to the church universal an understanding of the ways of God that are used by the church to this day.

When revival itself becomes our goal, it is seldom attained because it becomes an idol. Revival must never become an end in itself, but a means to an even higher end—the glory of the Lord being revealed and His kingdom being extended. Sometimes His kingdom is extended by other means than revival. Certainly we need more true revivals, but even those are founded upon simple obedience to whatever His plan may be, and His whole plan does not revolve just around revival. The day to day obedience of the church, and growing in true spiritual maturity, is just as important to the fulfillment of God's purposes as the great outbreaks of revival. When the cloud of His presence lifts and begins to move, we must be ready to move with Him. But when the cloud does not move, it is just as important that we rest in Him.

peae comes open the thought that
what you have done is about
to be frustrated.

# Chapter Five

# Unlikely Origins, Unlikely Heroes

R emarkably, the first known spark of the work of God
that became the Welsh Revival took place in Scranton,
Pennsylvania. A Welsh pastor with a thriving church was
thrilling his audiences with his oratory and intellect, when
suddenly he became broken before God and saw that he was
not a true prophet of the New Testament type. As he was
filled with remorse over his true state he came into a glorious
experience of the fullness of the Spirit. At once his preaching
changed—eloquence had been replaced by passion. He became burdened for his beloved Wales and resigned from his
church in Scranton to return to his homeland.

To the consternation of the religious people in Wales who
knew him before he left for America, the young minister
returned filled with a strange sense of urgency. No longer
did he preach for effect, to stir the congregation to great
emotional heights—he preached for results—the salvation
of souls and the awakening of the Lord's people. "It was,"
as one observer said, "indeed a strange thing to see Welsh
Preaching-festivals converted into what approximated very

nearly to Holiness Conventions when he was there! All believed in the sincerity of the preacher; most failed to explain him; many became definitely hostile."

This began in 1879. Even though this young preacher was being maligned and persecuted, he stayed on course, and soon began deeply affecting the other young ministers of his own denomination. The passion for the presence of God in these young men bound them into a holy fellowship that was to last for years to come. In the providence of God, early in 1903 these men found themselves occupying pulpits near each other so that their fellowship could continue. Their intensified desperation to have all that God had for them soon turned into a consciousness of the presence of God in their midst. These pastors began to note that after a period of agonizing intercession, the following day there would be unusual power for the preaching of the word. Glorious experiences beget more faith. Soon this little group of young ministers was convinced that something glorious was going to happen in their midst.

Dr. F.B. Meyer had been used in a wonderful way to minister to fellow preachers in South Wales, so they wrote to him and invited him to come and minister to them concerning the deep things of God. He replied that there would be a "Keswick Convention" at the beautiful Welsh spa of Llandridod Wells that year and invited them to attend, which they did. God moved on these young men mightily and they all came into an even deeper knowledge of the holy things of God. Looking back, many considered this convention to be another step up the mountain to the great transfiguration that was coming. There were other steps too. Those who have been a part of great awakenings or revivals could all look back and see a remarkable, carefully planned course that they had unknowingly followed.

In August, 1904, a second convention at Llandridod Wells took place. Dr. F.B. Meyer and Dr. A.T. Pierson ministered. Again the power and glory of God was in attendance. The Welsh saints were so overcome with the glory of God that they sang over and over the great chorus: "CROWN HIM LORD OF ALL"!

Meanwhile in Cardinganshire, in a tiny village named Ney Quay, the Lord had been quietly preparing other instruments for the coming awakening. The Rev. Joseph Jenkins had been deeply concerned about the lack of anointing in his own preaching, which compelled him to desperately seek a deeper life in Christ. Andrew Murray's book, *With Christ in the School of Prayer* came into his possession and moved him greatly at this time. He became increasingly burdened by the indifference among the Christians around him and the apathy of the young people in his own church. He exhorted them earnestly to obey the Spirit. This was in the early part of the year 1904.

## A Testimony Lights The Fire

The kindling was now ready, but the spark to light the fire would come from an even more unlikely source. In a Sunday morning prayer meeting for young people, Pastor Jenkins asked for testimonies of spiritual experiences. Several tried to speak on other subjects but the pastor stopped them. At last a young girl named Florrie Evans, who had been gloriously converted just a few days before, stood and with a trembling voice said: "I LOVE JESUS CHRIST—WITH ALL MY HEART"!

With these simple words the sparks that God had planted in so many hearts burst into flame and the great Welsh Revival began. The fire quickly spread to Blaenanerch, New Castle-Emlyn, Capel Drindod, and Twrgwin. Streams spread abroad like lava from a great volcano—soon multiplied thousands were aflame with the Holy Spirit's testimony of the glorious Son of God.

As the blessing in New Quay was quickly noised abroad, doors began to open on every hand. Led by their pastor, this group of young people, most of whom were between sixteen and eighteen years of age, conducted meetings throughout the south of the country. The fire continued to increase and lept over every boundary that tried to contain it. Conventions and conferences sprang up all over Wales, emphasizing holiness of heart and life in the Spirit. The Lord mightily used such men as W.S. Jones, E. Keri Evans, Jake Thickens, Seth and Frank Joshua, John Pugh, and R.B. Jones.

In August 1904, in the city of Cardiff, the famous evangelist R.A. Torrey held a service that resulted in many salvations. From every direction the Lord seemed to be bringing more fuel for the flames. In November of the same year, in Rhos, North Wales, the churches invited the esteemed preacher, R.B. Jones to conduct a campaign. He had entered into the Spirit-filled life the previous year and his entire ministry changed. He burned with a new message and news about him had been spreading throughout Britain. In God's proper timing, this flaming evangelist was added to the growing fire in Wales.

In Rhos the professing Christians were broken before God and began to remove the hindrances in their lives. They committed themselves to the full surrender to Christ and the reception of the Spirit in His fullness. The floodgates of heaven opened and the Spirit was poured out in torrents. The numbers grew until the churches overflowed nightly. Four weeks after Jones left Rhos, a Wrexham paper reported that "the whole district is in the grip of an extraordinary spiritual force which shows no sign of relaxing its hold."

Already the meetings were being carried on by the people themselves, sometimes with pastors present and sometimes without them. The meetings would start in the mornings and continue through the evenings. Then they began to spill over into the streets, into the homes, the trains, the factories and the mines. Soon great processions of awakened Christians and new converts were marching through the towns singing hymns and rejoicing in the Savior.

By this time there were approximately 40,000 believers who had become utterly desperate for God to pour out His Spirit in Wales. Most of these saints were yet unknown to each other and were scattered throughout the land, but the

Spirit was beginning to link them together in order to release one of the great demonstrations of the mighty power of God in answer to their prayers.

## The Light Shined In The Darkness

At this time the overall spiritual condition of Wales was as dark as it had ever been, and it seemed to be getting darker by the day. Bars flourished. Football (soccer), cock-fighting, prize fighting, gambling and prostitution seemed to have completely captured the soul of the working class. Murder, rape and other violent crimes were increasing dramatically and the authorities were close to losing what control they had.

The dark tunnels of the Welsh coal mines seemed a fitting symbol of what was happening to the country. But God was preparing a young, half-educated miner to be the outstanding voice to his generation. When he emerged from the mines to preach the gospel, Wales began to emerge from the dark pits of her sin. Soon this young miner, Evan Roberts, and his tiny country of Wales, would cause the whole world to pause and take notice of the wonderful works of God.

Evan Roberts was born on June 8, 1878, in a working-man's cottage called "Island House." It was a modest home with eight small rooms. For decades to come the neighbors would continually marvel at the pilgrims who would travel across continents to look at this little house and pray for the heavens to be opened again as they were for Evan.

Evan began work in the mines when he was just nine years old. His father, Henry, broke his leg in the pit, so his son had to help him in his job. After a few months, Evan himself took up the work of a door-boy whose duty was to look after the doors around the pit. He was paid seventy-five cents a week. Later he learned the trade of a blacksmith which he did in connection with the mine.

But Evan felt a burning passion to preach. Few who had other ambitions ever left the mines, even those who wanted

✱ to be preachers. Many have dreams but very few have turned their dreams into reality. Evan's pastor and friends encouraged him even though his lack of education made his prospects look very dim. But Evan persevered and, at twenty-six years of age, he entered the preparatory school at Newcastle Emlyn to prepare himself for the Trevecca College entrance examination. Evan had determined to do all that he could and to trust God to do the rest. Evan would never finish school, but many schools would one day devote their attention to studying Evan and the extraordinary move of God that he helped to lead. The Lord did not need Evan's knowledge—He only needed a willing vessel.

For a period of time Evan had been seeking and finding a more intimate relationship with the Lord. William Davies, a deacon at the Moriah Chapel, had counseled young Evan never to miss the prayer meetings in case the Holy Spirit would come and he would be missing. So Evan faithfully attended the Monday evening meeting at Moriah, Tuesday at Pisgah, Wednesday at Moriah, and Thursday and Friday at other prayer meetings and Bible classes. For thirteen years he did this and faithfully prayed for a mighty visitation of the Holy Spirit.

## The Revelation

One day before school, in the spring of 1904, Evan found himself in what he later referred to as a Mount of Transfiguration experience. The Lord revealed Himself in such an amazing and overwhelming manner that Evan was filled with divine awe. After this he would go through periods of uncontrollable trembling that brought concern to his family. For weeks God visited Evan each night. When his family pressed him to tell about the experiences he would only say it was something indescribable. When the time drew near for him to enter Grammar School at New Castle Emlyn, he was afraid to go because he was afraid that he would miss these encounters with the Lord.

At this time a convention was being held at Blaenanerch a few miles from his school. An evangelist named Seth Joshua was leading the meetings. On Thursday morning, September 29, 1904, Evan Roberts and nineteen other young people, including his friend Sydney Evans, attended the meeting. On the way to the meeting the Lord moved on the small company and they began to sing: "It is coming, it is coming - the power of the Holy Ghost - I receive it - I receive it - the power of the Holy Ghost."

During the seven o'clock meeting Evan was deeply moved and he broke down completely at the close of the service. When the Seth Joshua used the words "BEND US, OH LORD," Evan entered such travail that he heard nothing more. He later testified that the Spirit of God whispered to him: "This is what you need."

"Bend me, Oh Lord," he cried. But the fire did not fall. At the 9 o'clock meeting the spirit of intercession was moving on the congregation in great power. Evan was bursting to pray. Then the Spirit of God told him to do so publicly. With tears streaming down his face Evan just began to cry: "BEND ME! BEND ME! BEND ME! BEND US". Then the Holy Spirit came upon him with a mighty baptism that filled Evan with Calvary's love and a love for Calvary. That night the message of the cross was so branded upon Evan's heart that there would be no other theme of the great revival he would soon help lead. From that night on Evan Roberts could focus on one thought—the salvation of souls. Historians would refer to that night as "Blaenanerch's great meeting."

One midnight shortly after this, Evan's roommate and closest friend, Sydney Evans, came into the room to find Evan's face shining with a holy light. Astonished, he asked what had happened. Evan replied that he had just seen in a vision the whole of Wales being lifted up to heaven. He then prophesied: "We are going to see the mightiest revival that Wales has ever known—and the Holy Spirit is coming just now. We must get ready. We must have a little band and go all over the country preaching." Suddenly he stopped and with piercing eyes he cried: "DO YOU BELIEVE THAT GOD CAN GIVE US 100,000 SOULS, NOW?"

The presence of the Lord so gripped Sydney that he could not help but believe. Later, while sitting in a chapel, Evan saw in a vision some of his old companions and many other young people as a voice spoke to him saying: "GO TO THESE PEOPLE". He said, "Lord, if it is Thy will, I will go". Then the whole chapel became filled with light so dazzling that he could only faintly see the minister in the pulpit. He was deeply disturbed and wanted to make sure that this vision was of the Lord. He consulted with his tutor who encouraged him to go.

## They Obeyed Him

On October 31 Evan returned to his home by train having little knowledge of the great work of preparation that the Holy Spirit had already accomplished before him. His mother met him at the door and exclaimed in great surprise, "Where have you been? Why are you not at school? Are you ill!"

"No", he replied.

"Then why have you come back home?"

"Oh Mother, the Spirit has sent me back here to work among our own young people at the chapel at Moriah." Then turning to Dan, his younger brother, he said, "You shall see that there will be a great change at Loughor in less than a fortnight. We are going to have the greatest revival that Wales has ever seen".

Evan then went straight to his pastor and asked permission to hold services for young people. On that night, after the adult prayer meeting, he asked the young people to stay behind as he wanted to speak to them. Sixteen adults and only one little girl stayed. After the initial blast of disappointment, Evan began to explain in a quiet voice his reason for coming home. He said that he was simply obeying the Holy Spirit, and here at Moriah large numbers of young people were going to be saved. And above all, a mighty revival was coming to Wales!

This is how the most important meetings in the history of Wales began. There was a cold spirit and unbelief was so thick it seemed to hang in the air. The results were so disappointing that Evan could not help but be tempted to think that his visions were some strange delusion. It was a test much like that which the children of Israel endured after leaving Egypt. They were promised a land flowing with milk and honey and the first place to which they were taken did not even have water. When they finally came to a well, the water was bitter! Would the young preacher believe the visions or the voices that were now telling him that he had been duped by illusions of grandeur? It is at this point that many stray from the course that leads to the fulfillment of their callings. Would Evan?

No. He determined that he would rather be the greatest fool in Wales than miss a possible opportunity to see revival in Wales—Evan chose to stand by the vision just as he had prophesied. Within two weeks Loughor was changed and the first of 100,000 young people began streaming to the Lord. Because Evan did not despise the day of small beginnings he was used to start one of the greatest moves of God of all time.

# Chapter Six

# The Course Is Set

After the disappointing service with the young people, the next day's services were held at Pisgah, a small chapel nearby that was a mission of Moriah. This was a Tuesday night and strangely the audience had significantly increased. Evan spoke on the importance of being filled with the Spirit. This meeting lasted until 10 p.m.

## The Four Tenets

The next day, on November 2, Evan was back at Moriah and he spoke on *The Four Great Tenets*. This was to become the foundational message of the revival as they later became known as "The Four Points." These were the four essential conditions that Evan believed were required before revival could come. They were:

I.  All sin must be confessed to God and repented of. The church has to be cleansed—the Lord's bride would be without spot so there would be no room for compromise with sin. If there is anything in our lives about which there is even doubt as to whether it is good or evil—then cast it off!

**39**

II. There must be no cloud between the believer
and God. Have you forgiven *everybody*? If not,
don't expect forgiveness for your own sins. The
Scripture is clear, we cannot be forgiven until
we have forgiven. Unforgiveness separates us
from God.

III. We must obey the Holy Spirit. Do what the
Spirit prompts you to do. Prompt, implicit,
unquestioning obedience to the Spirit is required if we are going to be used by Him.

IV. There must be public confessions of Christ as
Savior. This is not just a one time incident after
our salvation experience or baptism—for the
Christian it is a way of life. (Evan also believed
that there was a difference between confession
and profession).

It was unknown to Evan when he first preached them, but
these "Four Tenets" set the direction for the revival, and
helped to keep it on course for its duration. They established
a foundation of repentance and then built upon a personal,
living relationship with the Lord. The driving force behind
the revival was not a doctrine, or a human personality, but
the Holy Spirit who had come to convict the world of sin,
and then to lead the world to the Forgiver of sin, Jesus Christ.
The Holy Spirit remained and moved powerfully for as long
as He was able to do this work in the simplicity required for
it.

On November 3 Evan met again at Moriah and taught the
children to pray "Send the Holy Spirit to Moriah for Jesus'
sake". He spoke that evening on "Ask, and it shall be given
you". "These things must be believed", he said "if the work
is to succeed. We must believe that God is willing and able
to answer our prayers. We must believe in a conquering
Christ who is able to defeat all opposition." Evan was compelled to press the point with more boldness than he had ever
felt before.

Now the vision was becoming more real to Evan than anything that his natural eyes could yet see. He felt the power of the creative word of God that could say: "Let there be light" when there was none. Evan was strangely confident that just by speaking it, it would happen. He did not understand all about prophecy, but that was not necessary. Understanding all about electricity is not a prerequisite for turning on the switch. Evan was going to keep prophesying until the light came.

On the next evening, after speaking for awhile, Evan threw the meeting open for prayer and testimony. The presence of the Lord was there and the meeting lasted until midnight.

It was announced that the next meeting would be for young people, but that evening just as many adults crowded into the chapel. There was a strange expectation in the air that God was going to do something marvelous and no one could bear to stay away. When God is not moving meetings are a burden, but just as in the Book of Acts, when God is moving all the people want to do is meet together. The youth meetings were now attracting just as many fathers and mothers. Many of the children began to have wonderful conversions, astonishing their elders. Evan spoke from Ephesians 5:18, on not being drunk with wine but being filled with the Holy Spirit. Again the meeting lasted past midnight.

In less than a week the meetings had gone from being cold and powerless to a level that neither the young preacher nor the people had witnessed before. Days before it seemed that Evan's words just fell to the floor. Now his words had the power to penetrate even the hardest heart and genuine repentance was rolling over the people like waves. Evan's vision was being fulfilled before his eyes.

On Sunday, November 6, a visiting clergyman from another town occupied the morning pulpit. Evan sat and listened to the message. The pastor, wanting to give Evan an opportunity to obey God in what he had seen, announced that Evan would preach in the evening. Evan's subject was "The Importance of Obedience."

In his message, Evan personalized the Holy Spirit and gave the meeting into His hands. The Holy Spirit came and sixty young people responded for salvation. Evan then exhorted the people to pray: "Send the Spirit now for Christ's sake!" This meeting also lasted well past midnight and news of it spread throughout the whole of Loughor. The spirit of the people had gone from unbelief to hope, to expectation, to awe. It seemed that each night an unseen hand was turning up a spiritual thermostat a few more degrees. The prophecy was now becoming history.

## The Test

The Monday evening prayer meetings would never be considered one of the highlights of the Moriah Chapel services. Like most congregational prayer meetings, there were a handful of regular attenders and a few who might occasionally drop in. On Monday, November 7, the chapel was packed all the way back to the door. This had never happened before in the history of the chapel. At 8 o'clock Evan Roberts arrived, opened his Bible and read from the last chapter of Malachi:

> **"But unto you that fear my name shall the Sun of righteousness arise with healing in his wings; and ye shall go forth, and grow up as calves of the stall. And ye shall tread down the wicked; for they shall be as ashes under the soles of your feet in the day that I shall do this, saith the Lord of hosts."**
> **(Malachi 4:2,3, KJV)**

Then Evan astonished those in attendance by boldly declaring that this Scripture was going to be fulfilled immediately in Wales!

When the Lord first read from the prophecy in Isaiah in His own synagogue at Nazareth, those who heard Him were likewise astonished at His boldness. The Lord spoke with an authority that required all who heard to either believe Him or reject Him. They chose to reject Him. Those who heard Evan Roberts that night in Moriah were challenged in the same way by his boldness. For a few brief moments this great move of God hung in the balance. Here was the young man they had known from childhood, had worked with in the mines, and now he was declaring the word of God with a boldness that they had never before witnessed. Evan had spoken in such a way that they were either going to have to believe God for a marvelous and unprecedented revival, or reject the messenger. They chose to believe. Another major hurdle was passed; the spiritual atmosphere in Wales had reached its critical mass. Now revival to at least some degree was inevitable.

## They Received His Messengers

Could it be possible that this entire revival depended on the reception of this one man? Yes! If we believe both the Biblical and historic precedents of revival, it is likely that the great Welsh Revival depended on the reception of the messenger the Lord had chosen to strike the match on the prepared fuel. One of the greatest Biblical revivals took place in the wicked, heathen city of Nineveh because they chose to believe the most unlikely, wayward, Hebrew prophet—Jonah. Our reception of the grace of God is often dependent on our ability to let Him use the foolish to confound the wise, the weak to confound the strong. The Lord Jesus Himself, before His departure from this realm declared that: "**... from now on you shall not see Me until you say, '*Blessed is He who comes in the name of the Lord*'**" (Matthew 23:39). By this He was declaring that from that time on we would not see Him unless we blessed those that He sent to us.

The Welsh Revival is one of the classic examples of how a people heard the Lord when He knocked on their door, how they opened to Him, and were able to experience His presence for a period of time. Many revivals have begun only to be quickly short-circuited by ambitious men who tried to use them for their own purposes. Many others never got started because men, overreacting to the selfishly ambitious, rejected the messengers the Lord sent to them.

It is right that we desire to see God receive the glory, but this does not mean that men should not get any attention or recognition. One of the great ironies of church history is that those who are the most zealous for seeing that men do not steal God's glory almost never experience a true move of God, because they reject the messengers He sends to them. Paul was bold to defend his recognition as an apostle because he could not rightly minister to the churches unless they recognized the purpose for which he had come to them.

We must receive a prophet *in the name of a prophet* if we are going to receive a prophet's reward. If we receive a prophet as just a teacher, or a brother, we will miss what God could have given to us. The same is true of every ministry. We must receive a pastor as a pastor if we are going to receive the reward of his ministry. The same is true of an evangelist, teacher or apostle. We must recognize the gift of God in the messenger to receive the gift that God is sending to us.

To receive the gift of God in another is to recognize the work and purpose of God in them. This is a demonstration of the humility required to receive the grace of God, because **"God resists the proud, but gives His grace to the humble"** (James 4:6). It takes humility to receive the message of God from another man, especially one that we have known for awhile. It is this humility that God is looking for so that He can trust us with His grace. The greater the humility, the greater the grace. Nineveh showed extraordinary humility and received extraordinary grace. First century Israel showed extraordinary spiritual pride by rejecting the very One who had created them, and thereby received the destruction that Ninevah had avoided.

Our tendency to police the body of Christ in order to see that others are not exalting themselves is a terrible form of spiritual pride; this often causes us to miss the grace of God by rejecting those that He has sent to us as His provision. The apostle Paul commended the Galatians for receiving him "as an angel from God" even though his flesh was a trial to them. The people of Wales demonstrated what may have been an unprecedented humility by receiving one who had grown up right in their midst as a prophet from God. The result of this humility was a commensurate outpouring of God's grace, a grace so great that it caused the whole world to marvel.

There is a delicate balance between wrongly exalting men, and receiving them properly. The Lord said that as we do to the least of His little ones we have done it unto Him. When men receive the ambassador of a nation with honor they are honoring that nation. To not receive him with the proper protocol is to dishonor that nation. How much more should we receive the Lord's ambassadors with honor? There is a difference between properly honoring someone and worshipping them.

The Lord honors men and He exalts them. In fact, He promised to exalt them: **"... for everyone who exalts himself shall be humbled, but he who humbles himself** *shall be exalted"* **(Luke 18:14).** James said, **"Humble yourselves in the presence of the Lord,** *and He will exalt you"* **(James 4:10).** It is our job to humble ourselves, it is God's job to do the exalting, and He is clear that if we try to do His job He will do our job. However, he did not say that we were supposed to humble others! That is one of the most basic forms of pride! To find the correct balance between properly honoring the messengers that God sends to us, without worshipping them, is indeed a crucial issue.

In Wales, for a short period of time, the church seemed to find this perfect balance. The people not only honored the primary evangelists, they honored even the most humble saints whom the Lord had chosen to use. During the time of this revival they were quick to recognize and receive the gift of God regardless of the messenger. The primary evangelists were so committed to humbling themselves that both the Lord and the people were able to honor them properly. They used the attention that they were given to direct the people to the Lord. Men who are truly used by the Holy Spirit are not looking for honor or attention, but it will come, and they must have the grace to handle it properly when it does.

## The Presence Comes

Almost everyone in attendance at the meeting on Monday night, November 7, was moved to tears; many cried in agony. By midnight the presence of the Lord was so intense that it could hardly be contained. The people had never experienced such deep repentance, or such deep joy. Those crying in remorse for their sins could not be distinguished from those crying in ecstasy at the nearness of God. It was after 3 a.m. before an attempt to close the meeting was possible.

The next evening the people crowded into the chapel early just to be able to get seats. Everyone was talking about another great awakening, maybe even another Pentecost! But that night the meeting was cold and lifeless. Evan and a few faithful remained until almost 3 a.m. agonizing in prayer. Why had the Lord departed so quickly? About 6 a.m. Evan and Dan finally left to go home and sleep.

Upon arriving home they were jolted by cries of "I'm dying! I'm dying!" coming from their mother. Discouraged, she had left the meeting early the night before. Now she was crying out in agony declaring that she felt the entire weight of Calvary on her soul. Evan quickly recognized her burden and began to pray with her. Later she explained that after leaving the meeting the night before she began to feel the agony of the Lord as He had endured the cold, hardness of Gethsemane which even His own disciples would not bear with Him. She felt that her leaving the chapel at such a critical time to go home and sleep had been the same rejection of an opportunity to stand with the Lord. She was devastated. Evan was wise. He did not try to comfort her—he tried to help her repent.

The Holy Spirit was working on the others in the community in the same way. The Lord had in fact been at the meeting, but had come in a form that they did not recognize.

The Lord does not always come to excite us—at times He comes in silence and demands silence. Sometimes He does not want to speak to us as much as He wants us to learn to just wait. The people of Loughor got the message quickly. Now it was time for Evan to be astonished at the people.

Just as Evan and his brother were trying to fall asleep they were awakened by a strange noise in the streets. It was just 6:00 a.m. but the streets were noisy with crowds on their way to the early morning prayer services! The entire population of the town had responded in repentance just as Evan's mother, and was being transformed into a praying multitude who would not fall asleep in the presence of the Lord again for a very long time. Had anything like this ever happened before?

# Chapter Seven

# Spontaneous Combustion

On November 9 and 10 Evan Roberts preached at the Brynteg Congregational chapel. By the second night the entire congregation was, in the words of James E. Stewart, "completely carried away by spiritual emotion."

On this day the first public reference to the Revival was made in a secular newspaper. Soon the entire press in Wales was devoted almost exclusively to covering this amazing revival. Then almost every major newspaper in the world picked up the story. The following is the short article that appeared in *The Western Mail* of Cardiff, Wales.

---

### Great Crowds Of People Drawn To Loughor
*Congregations Stay Till Half-past-two In The Morning*

A remarkable religious revival is now taking place at Loughor. For some days a young man named Evan Roberts, a native of Loughor, has been causing great surprise at Moriah Chapel. The place has been besieged by dense crowds of people unable to obtain

**48**

admission. Such excitement has prevailed that the road on which the chapel is situated has been lined with people from end to end. Roberts, who speaks in Welsh, opens his discourse by saying that he does not know what he is going to say but that when he is in communion with the Holy Spirit, the Holy Spirit will speak, and he will simply be the medium of His wisdom. The preacher soon launches out into a fervent and, at times, impassioned oration. His statements have had stirring effects upon his listeners. Many who have disbelieved Christianity for years are again returning to the fold of their younger days. One night, so great was the enthusiasm invoked by the young revivalist that, after his sermon which lasted two hours, the vast congregation remained praying and singing until two-thirty in the morning! Shopkeepers are closing early in order to get a place in the chapel, and tin and steel workers throng the place in their working clothes.

On November 11 the Moriah was teeming with over 800 people trying to squeeze into the little chapel. A young girl in her early teens seemed to capture the feeling when she cried out, "Oh, what will Heaven be like if it is so wonderful down here!"

By the next day the prayer meetings had so overflowed the chapel that people were opening their homes for meetings throughout the city. By early afternoon wagons and carts were pouring into the town from all over the countryside. By night even the home prayer meetings were overflowing as crowds stood outside many of them straining to hear what was going on inside. The evangelists were running from chapel to chapel and house to house. Salvation seemed to be flowing down the streets like a great flood. On this day Sam Jenkins, the famous gospel singer, was first heard in the revival. In one of the galleries he broke out in the song "Saved By Grace" and the multitude picked it up, singing it over and over. On this night, the great hymn

"Throw Out The Lifeline" was also sung for the first time in the revival.

The meetings lasted until after 5 a.m. that Sunday morning. Evan introduced his friend Sydney to the throngs at Loughor and then departed for Aberdare without sleeping. The grocery shops were completely cleared of food as the people who had come from long distances determined that they were not going to go home. Feeling like they had found the cloud of glory, they were simply not going to leave it.

## The Meetings In Aberdare

On Sunday morning, November 13, Evan Roberts and five young ladies between the ages of eighteen and twenty (Priscilla Watkins, Mary Davies, Livina Hooker, Annie M. Rees, and Anne Davies) were driven to meet the train at Swansea for Aberdare. These young girls were from nearby Gorseinon and had each been baptized in the Holy Spirit. They were about to carry the flame of revival all over Britain during the next eighteen months.

The opening meeting that Sunday in Aberdare was a disappointment. The local Christians criticized the youthfulness of the revival party and it seemed that the Spirit was grieved. Even so, the young evangelists were not easily defeated. They were convinced that God had sent them to Aberdare and only God could send them away.

On the next evening one thousand people crowded into the Ebenezer Congregational Chapel. Still there was no sign that the Lord was doing anything special. The next day almost the entire town stayed home from work to attend the morning prayer meeting. Inexplicably, with no one knowing how they were told, huge crowds were coming from all directions. Anticipation was reaching a fever pitch even though nothing special had yet happened.

In the evening service, Evan Roberts circulated a hymn which was to become one of the great hymns of the revival: *Heavenly Jesus, ride victorious, Gird Thy sword upon Thy thigh.*

There was a spontaneous outburst of worship, prayer and praise. When this meeting was reaching its spiritual peak, Evan prophesied with great authority that a mighty revival was coming to *all* of Wales and they were only opening the gates for it. Before the meetings in Aberdare were to end all of Britain would know that the Holy Spirit had indeed come to Wales.

## The Revival Spreads

From Aberdare Evan travelled to over two dozen cities and towns throughout Wales. In every place the dry wood had been prepared and he simply cast the spark that would set it ablaze. The awe of the Lord was upon everyone and His presence was felt everywhere. Spontaneous prayer meetings began in the mines, factories, schools and shops. Even the amusement parks were filled with a holy awe as brigades of evangelists swept through them. Men who entered taverns to order drinks left them untouched as conviction and the fear of God came upon them.

Wave after wave of the Holy Spirit was passing over the land. The degree to which this move was affecting society could be seen in the way that it impacted the favorite Welsh sport, football (soccer). At the time the Revival broke out the whole nation was nearly in a frenzy over the sport. Working class men seemed to think and talk about this one obsession. Gambling on the games was rampant. Then the star football players were converted and joined the open-air street meetings to testify of the glorious things that the Lord had done for them. Soon the players were so captivated with the Lord that they lost interest in the games, the teams disbanded; the stadiums were empty.

This miracle could only be compared to turning on your television set one Sunday afternoon to watch a National Football League game, only to hear the announcers trying to explain that none of the players had shown up because they were out evangelizing the city, and none of the fans had shown up because they were out there too! No one preached against sport or football—the people had simply become so passionate for the Lord that, for a season, such games just could no longer interest either the players or the people.

The degree to which Wales was impacted by this revival in such a short period of time probably does not have a counterpart anywhere in history. It was almost as if the nation had been converted in a day, and not just converted—transformed! As the news spread about what was happening, men and women came from the far corners of the earth to witness it, and it does not seem that any were disappointed by what they found. Many testified of being profoundly impacted by the presence of the Lord as soon as they touched the soil of this little principality. Even letters and telegrams from Wales seemed to carry the fire—as they were read souls would be saved and revival would break out. No one had ever even heard of anything like this before—and it was just beginning!

# Chapter Eight

# The Silent Week

F or three months before the outburst of revival in Loughor, Evan Roberts had slept little as he interceded for his beloved Wales and sought a deeper communion with the Lord. During the months following the outbreak he could scarcely find time to eat or sleep—thousands of hungry new believers followed him everywhere he went. When we have taken the Lord's yoke and are working with Him, our labor actually refreshes us instead of tiring us and we are able to experience superhuman endurance. But even the Lord rested after His work, and He established a principle that we should take regular rests from our labors. Evan had been going without rest for months, violating this principle. By the end of February, 1905, he was near exhaustion.

However, God did not rest on the seventh day because He was weary; "**The Everlasting God, the Lord, the Creator of the ends of the earth does not become weary or tired**" (Isaiah 40:28). Neither does He call man to observe Sabbaths simply for a cessation of labor, but rather for the purpose of drawing near to Him from whom our true sustenance comes. At this time the Spirit revealed to Evan that he must have a week of silence. On February 22, Evan revealed that he was not going to preach at Briton Ferry, where he had an engagement. For the entire week He remained confined to his bedroom without speaking to anyone, not even his relatives. He was staying in the house of a Mr. and Mrs. Jones, who faithfully turned away hundreds of people, including famous preachers and newspaper men who had come from all over the world to see him.

This week of silence, just as the revival was reaching an unprecedented crescendo, amazed the world almost as much as the revival. How could the leader of such a move of God completely withdraw himself at its very peak? But Evan knew that he was not the source of the revival, and that if the presence of the Lord was removed it would all end regardless of how hard he and the other evangelists worked. Obedience is more important than sacrifice. Evan was willing to let the world's most famous preachers and reporters be offended rather than risk the Lord's displeasure. This is the foundation of true spiritual leadership. The greatest spiritual leader is the one who follows the Lord most closely.

## Four More Principles

Evan did not reveal publicly what took place in his encounters with the Lord that week, but everyone noticed that he emerged from this period of isolation with an even greater anointing. In the personal diary he kept during this time, Evan noted on the fifth day four simple principles to which he had to devote himself. They were, in his own words:

1) I must take great care, first, to do all that God says—commands—and that only. Moses lost himself here—struck the rock."

2) Second, to take every matter, however insignificant, to God in prayer. Joshua lost himself here: he made a covenant with the Gibeonites who pretended that they lived in a far-off country while they were living close at hand.

3) Third, to give obedience to the Holy Spirit.

4) Fourth, to give all the glory to Him.

On the sixth day of this week Evan noted in his diary a personal prophecy from the Lord:

"Lo, I am the Lord, who hath lifted thee up from the depth. I have sustained thee thus far. Lift up thine eyes and look on the fields and, behold, they are white. Shall I suffer thee to spread a table before Mine enemies? As I live, saith the Lord, the windows of heaven shall be opened, and the rain shall come down upon the parched earth. With flowers the wilderness shall yet be decked, and the meadow land shall be the habitation of kings. The ground shall sprout and blossom in its fullness and the heavens shall look down with laughter upon hidden riches on the earth, yielding glory unto God. Open thine hand, and I will fill it with power. Open thy mouth and I will fill it with wisdom. Open thy heart, and I will fill it with love. Look toward the west, and call thousands; toward the south, and say 'Come'; toward the north, and say 'Draw nigh.' Look towards the east, and say 'Let the sun arise and shed forth its warmth. Let life spring up. Let the nations which have rejected My name live.' To kings turn thyself and say, 'Bend'; To knights, 'Submit ye.' To the priests, 'Deal out judgment, pity, forgiveness.' Ye islands, seas, and kingdoms, give ear unto Me, I am the Almighty. Shall I lift up My rod over you? Did I not swear by the prophet Isaiah: 'I have sworn by myself, the word is gone out of My mouth in righteousness, and shall not return, that unto Me every knee shall bow, every tongue shall swear'?" (Isaiah 45:23)

## A Prophetic Sign

When Evan was later questioned by his friends concerning the principle object of what was called "The Silence", he explained: "It was not for the sake of my mind or my body to have a rest, but for *a sign*. When I asked the Lord what was the object of the seven days of silence He distinctly said, "As thy tongue was tied for seven days, so shall Satan be bound seven times."

Such prophetic signs are an enigma to the natural mind. When the king of Israel came to ask Elisha if he should fight against the Arameans, the prophet told him to strike the ground with his bow and arrows. When the king only struck the ground three times the prophet was mad, declaring that if the king had struck the ground five or six times he would have destroyed his enemies, but because he only struck the ground three times he would only defeat them three times (see II Kings 13:14-19). What did striking the ground with a bow and arrow have to do with the king's impending battles? Why were seven days of silence required of Evan Roberts for Satan to be bound seven times? The Spiritual realm is *much greater* than the natural realm. Obedience to even the most seemingly insignificant promptings of the Spirit can have consequences in the spiritual realm that the natural mind just cannot comprehend. Those who insist on understanding God's ways with their natural minds will trip over the spiritual stumbling blocks. The Lord warned us through Isaiah:

**"For My thoughts are not your thoughts, neither are your ways My ways," declares the Lord. For as the heavens are higher than the earth, so are My ways higher than your ways, and My thoughts than your thoughts." (Isaiah 55:8)**

Great moves of God require great obedience to the ways of the Spirit, but the flesh wars against the spirit and many can never overcome this hurdle. Only the Spirit can beget that which is Spirit. Evan Roberts did not have to dress for power. He violated almost every church growth principle. He was neither educated nor eloquent. The only thing that he had going for him was the anointing—but that was all that he needed! Those who trust in the Spirit are utterly dependent on the Spirit. If the Holy Spirit did not show up, Evan had nothing else to fall back on. He did not have a program he could resort to or leftover sermons he could warm up.

When we have only the Holy Spirit, then obedience to the Spirit is everything. Few have ever been so willing to trust in the Lord to this degree, and few have ever seen true revival because of it. If the Lord does not show up at our meetings we always have a pretty good program anyway. If the Lord completely departed from many churches they would not ever realize it. But those who have tasted of His presence can never again be satisfied merely with programs—they must have the Lord. Even though the hype, manipulation and programs have wearied the church to the degree that the Laodicean spirit of lukewarmness now pervades, there is a hunger for the Lord Himself that is beginning to rise in her. The church at the end of this age will return to her first love. She will be so compelled to draw near to Him, that He will draw near to her—on a scale that will signify that even this great Welsh Revival was but a foretaste of the harvest that is the end of the age.

# Chapter Nine

# God Uses Men

Almost every great revival or move of God in both Scripture and history was ignited by a single individual, but none of them were sustained by just one individual. The same was true in Wales. Almost everyone recognized that Evan Roberts was the principle individual used to both start and sustain the revival, but there were many others that were used to prepare the nation for it, and others still who fanned the flames throughout the nation. It was not the presence of Evan Roberts which brought revival, but the presence of God.

The greatest vessel that the Lord uses is still an "earthen vessel." Once we behold the glory of the Lord the vessel loses our attention. Compared to the Lord Jesus, even the great apostle Paul is a mere man, an empty vessel. But very few have ever risen above worshipping the temple of the Lord so that they can truly worship the Lord of the temple. The reporters and preachers who flocked to Wales from around the world all wanted to see Evan Roberts. Those who were a part of the revival hardly even noticed when Evan entered a meeting. They loved and respected him, but their hearts were captured by the glory of the Son of God. Because the people had fallen in love with the Lord, they therefore loved and honored His messengers, but they did not worship them. When we see the glory of the Son it is impossible to be overly impressed by men, whether they are kings, presidents, or even the greatest men of God.

Evan Roberts was a yielded vessel that the Lord could use, but so were a multitude of other pastors and evangelists who were used to reap a mighty harvest simultaneous with the ministry of Evan and Dan Roberts, Sydney Evans, Sam Jenkins and "The Singing Sisters." The revival spread to the uttermost points of Wales although the principal evangelists never visited there. The Welsh Revival is a study of the Lord's use of sovereign vessels, and how He sometimes chooses to move sovereignly without any vessels at all. The Lord never limited Himself to move only according to one plan.

## The Common Denominator

There was a conspicuous common denominator found everywhere that this revival broke out. It was that the Son of God was being lifted up and all men were being drawn to Him. Holiness and obedience were an emphasis, but it was primarily because the Son was holy and everyone wanted to please Him in all things. The presence of the Lord was so strong that no one could imagine speaking vile words or performing vile acts.

Those who were present could only describe His presence as being absolutely beyond description! The promptings of the Holy Spirit were so distinct that thousands would simultaneously spring to their feet to worship in such perfect unison that those who witnessed it considered it miraculous. At times the glory of the Lord would so shine from the pulpit that the evangelist or pastor would flee from it to keep from being completely overcome. Many testified that they could not stand the brightness of the glory of the Lord that came upon some meetings.

Thousands of young converts spread out all over the land preaching the good news they had found. They had no credentials or authority from men— all they had was the Holy Spirit and that was all they needed. The Book of Acts was happening all over again, and then some. Small children won many souls for Christ. New converts were leading large prayer meetings and Bible studies. At times Bible studies or prayer meetings being held in the same city would all empty into the streets at the same time, following an unseen Conductor, and march around the town together singing praises to the Lord until the early morning hours.

The largest and most influential newspapers were soon almost completely dominated by news of the revival. Headlines of crime, violence and scandal were replaced by conversion counts, news from the meetings, the words to new hymns and revival maps detailing where the Spirit was moving with the greatest intensity. The advertisements for liquor disappeared and the large advertisements were all bought by Christian publishers trying to keep up with the need for Bibles and hymn books.

The following reports were compiled by James E. Stewart from a newspaper under the heading *Doings Of The Churches* and published in his book *Invasion Of Wales By The Spirit* (Revival Literature, pages 52-57):

> BLAENAVON. On Saturday evening a band of young lads between the age of 14 and 16 held prayer meetings in the different places in the principle streets.

> DOWLAIS. At a recent prayer meeting, attended by no fewer than 214 persons, the proceedings resolved themselves into a huge Bible class. This great interest in the Holy Scriptures is the result of the present revival.

> BRYNCETHIN. The services have now been held here nightly for fifteen weeks and a large number of converts have been added to the Free Churches. For the sake of educating the young converts it has been decided to have a Bible class for two nights in

every week and these classes are very largely attended.

RHOS. Visitors to the revival meeting continue to pour in from the Lake District; Birkenhead, Liverpool, and the adjoining districts.

TREMADOC. The revival has had and continues to have a marked effect here. The chapels have been overflowing up to two and three o'clock in the morning.

NEWBRIDGE. An official of the Colynen colliery, when asked how the religious fervor had expressed itself underground, said: "This is a blessed time. When I go around on my inspection now I rarely hear a blasphemous word of oath. There is a glorious change for the better."

CARDIGAN. A meeting in the Tabernacle Calvinist Methodist Church where the Rev. Seth Joshua was conducting a mission was prolonged till after midnight. It was a wonderful gathering and will long be remembered for the outpouring of the Holy Spirit. Most of the 1200 people present were on their knees simultaneously and they remained in this attitude for about 2 hours and many persons are known to have accepted Christ.

HOLYHEAD. In this important town a drunken man is a thing of the past and the police are having an easy time of it. 500 converts have been reported.

PONTYPOOL. The missionary enthusiasm is running high amongst the 200 converts at the Tabernacle and at a recent meeting it was decided to divide them into groups and to hold services at different cottages. Street disturbances have become conspicuous by their absences and the fact that there has not been a single fight at the bottom of High Street, which is always regarded as the "prize ring of Pontypool", is put down to the good influences of the Revival.

COEDBOETH. This quiet neighborhood has felt a strong spiritual visitation for the past three months. The total number of converts is now 210 and many more are expected. There have been united prayer meetings three nights a week and on the rest of the evenings each church holds meetings at its own place of worship. Remarkable scenes have been witnessed. The women have daily prayer meetings, morning and evening. Young men and young women are preaching in the open air with great success and many drunkards have been converted. The life of whole churches has been reformed.

BLAENAVON. All the churches in the town recently had a combined procession through the streets and now a second parade has been arranged.

BERTILLERY. As the result of the special week of meetings there have been about 1500 converts.

BRITHOIR. A meeting near the railway station — the continuation of a previous prayer meeting — was attended by many persons from clubs and public houses and continued till near midnight. Then they went to the nearby Chapel and the gathering broke up at 2 a.m.

AMMANFORD. Half a dozen young people cannot meet accidently in the street without joining in praise. Recently a group of children met on The Cross and began to sing and pray. Ultimately they were joined by men and women and the result was a grand open air prayer meeting. Ammanford is a new town. Young people, full of enthusiasm, frequently walk three or four miles over the mountains to villages, farms and hamlets to hold meetings.

TREHARRIS. At Brynhyfrd Welsh Baptist, forty candidates were recently baptized making a total of 138 Baptisms. 220 have recently been saved in this church.

RHONDDA VALLEY. A scene which may be witnessed any morning in dozens of pits in South Wales is carried out every morning here at 5 a.m. Scores of miners hold a service before going home from the midnight shift. The Superintendent starts a hymn, "In the deep and mighty ocean", and then the pit re-echoes the song. An old man whose grey head is tinged with coal dust falls on his knees to pray. Others do the same. The service attracts men from different workings and flickering lights are seen approaching the improvised temple. "Now, boys, those of you who love Christ, UP WITH YOUR LAMP!" cries a young miner. In a second, scores of lights flicker in the air and another song of thanks sets the mine ringing.

ABERTILLERY (again). The work goes on. Great things have taken place in the Salvation Army Hall but services are held nightly in practically every chapel in the neighborhood. There are now 2500 converts.

ANGLESEY. The Isle of Anglesey has been stirred from end to end by the revival. At the 55 Methodist chapels there have been 1116 converts, 276 at 15 Independent chapels, 366 at the 24 Baptist places of worship and 116 at the 8 Wesleyan Churches, making a total of 1,673 converts for the 102 chapels.

CARNARVON. A score of volunteer missionaries numbering 150 from the local churches of the town have undertaken house to house visitation to invite the people to come to the churches.

REVIVAL FERVOUR IN DURHAM, (England). Revival fervor still spreads in North West Durham in the North of England. Those connected with the cause for a long period remember no such general awakening during the last 20 years. There has been an upheaval which has been the general topic of conversation throughout the whole district. All over Durham marvelous scenes are taking place and the chapels are packed every night with souls being saved.

GARW VALLEY. Underground meetings are being held in nearly all the collieries. The early converts are among the most ardent workers and their efforts are proving very successful. At one of these underground meetings, no fewer than 36 men surrendered themselves to Christ.

GARNDIFFAITH. At Pisgah 40 conversions are recorded. A man 70 years of age stood up and confessed Christ as his Savior. Although late, he felt that he was glad that he had at last found peace and joy. A young man had been praying for his father and he asked that his petition might be answered that night. Just then his father came to the meeting and made a full surrender. A man who had been a great drunkard and blasphemer and who had starved his wife and children by missing his work for weeks at the time, found his way into one of the meetings and, with tears streaming from his eyes, he cried aloud for forgiveness. He prayed that God might find a way to his wife's heart and she, too, soon cried for pardon. Shouts of praise and joy were raised.

GLYNNEATH. The two independent churches ADDOLDY AND CAPEL-Y-GLYN which had been on unbrotherly terms for a period of nearly twelve years have been reconciled and united meetings have been held. The two ministers shook hands before a united church of nearly 400 members.

HAFOD. Underground prayer meetings at the Trevor pit have been conducted by Mr. W. Rogers who is known as the converted footballer.

PENTRE. The ministers of all the chapels recently exchanged pulpits for a day with the idea of breaking down denominationalism.

MAESTEG. An insurance agent told a reporter that at practically every house he called at after Christmas he was met by the wife with a happy smile and these words, "This is the happiest Christmas we have ever had." Their husbands had been converted and stopped their wastage of money in gambling and drunkenness.

CARNARVON. Details have just reached us of wonderful meetings. The influence of the Holy Spirit is felt most powerfully by men and women alike. Strong men pale and tremble. Young men and women storm the gates of heaven with overwhelming importunity and overpowering effect. The whole congregation is completely melted into pronounced weeping and sobbing. Large numbers are finding the Lord. Two well known reprobates came forward and sank on their knees and began to beat their breasts.

The Bible Society's records show that over three times the number of Bibles are now being sold since the revival broke out. The booksellers say it is no trouble now to sell Bibles; the trouble is to get them.

A lovely story is told of a child of four in an infant class who held up his hand to call the teacher's attention.

"Well?", inquired the teacher, "What is it?"

Swift and telling came the words, "Please, teacher, do you love Jesus?"

The arrow reached its mark. There and then the teacher came to the Lord and she later went out to India as a missionary.

Someone overheard one child ask another, "Do you know what has happened at Rhos?"

"No, I don't, except that Sunday comes every day now!"

"Don't you know?"

"No, I don't."

"Why, Jesus Christ has come to live in Rhos, now."

Winkey Pratney found and recorded the following newspaper report in his book *Revival* (Whitaker House, pages 190-191):

The scene is almost indescribable. Tier upon tier of men and women filled every inch of space. Those who could not gain admittance stood outside and listened at the doors. Others rushed to the windows where almost every word was audible. When at 7:00 the service began quite 2,000 people must have been present. The enthusiasm was unbounded. Women stood and shouted till perspiration ran down their faces, and then jumped up one after another to testify. One told in quivering accents the story of a drunken life. A working collier spoke like a practiced orator; one can imagine what a note the testimony of a converted gypsy woman struck when, dressed in her best, she told of her reformation and repentance. At ten o'clock the meeting had lost none of its ardor. Prayer after prayer went up...time and again the four ministers who stood in the pulpit attempted to start a hymn, but it was all in vain. The revival has taken hold of the people, and even Mr. Roberts cannot keep it in check. His latest convert is a policeman who, after complaining that the people had gone mad after religion so there was nothing to do, went to see for himself, and bursting into tears, confessed the error of his ways and repented.

William T. Stead, the editor of the famous *Pall Mall Gazette* was thought by some to be the most powerful man in Britain at the time. He made a personal visit to the revival and the *London Methodist Times* recorded the following interview with him upon his return (published in *The Great Revival In Wales*, Shaw, page 56):

"Well, Mr. Stead, you've been to the revival. What do you think of it?"

"Sir," Mr. Stead replied, "the question is not what I think of it, but what it thinks of me, of you, and all the rest of us. For it is a very real thing, this revival, a live thing which seems to have a power and a grip which may get hold of a good many of us who at present are mere spectators."

"Do you think it is on the march then?"

"A revival is something like a revolution, It is apt to be wonderfully catching."

"You speak as if you dreaded the revival coming your way."

"No, that is not so. Dread is not the right word. Awe expresses my sentiment better. For you are in the presence of the unknown. You have read ghost stories and can imagine what you would feel if you were alone at midnight in the haunted chamber of some old castle and you heard the slow and stealthy step stealing along the corridor where the visitor from another world was said to walk. If you go to South Wales and watch the revival you will feel pretty much just like that. There is something there from the other world. You cannot say whence it came or whither it is going, but it moves and lives and reaches for you all the time. You see men and women go down in sobbing agony before your eyes as the invisible Hand clutches at their heart. And you shudder. It is pretty grim I tell you, if you are afraid of strong emotions, you'd better give the revival a wide berth."

"But is it all emotion? Is there no teaching?"

"Precious little. Do you think teaching is what people want in revival? These people, all the people in a land like ours are taught to death, preached to insensibility. They all know the essential truths. They know they are not living as they ought to live, and no amount of teaching will add anything to that conviction."

"Then I take it your net impressions have been favorable?"

"How could they be otherwise? Did I not feel the pull of that unseen Hand? Have I not heard the glad outburst of melody that hailed the confession of some who in a very truth had found salvation? Of course it is all very much like what I have seen in the Salvation Army. And I was delighted to see that at last the Welsh churches are recognizing the equal ministry of men and women... There is a wonderful spontaneity about all, and so far its fruits have been good and only good."

"Will it last?"

"Nothing lasts forever in this mutable world...But if the analogy of all previous revivals holds good, this religious awakening will be influencing for good the lives of numberless men and women who will be living and toiling and carrying on with this God's world of ours long after you and I have been gathered to our fathers."

Even the most powerful politicians, statesmen, intellectuals and rival religious leaders had difficulty denying the impact of the revival on the entire principality of Wales. Debts were paid, stolen goods returned, and the taverns were forsaken and closed. A serious problem developed at the mines because the horses had been trained to respond to the curses of the drivers, and since drivers did not curse anymore, the horses could not understand their commands!

Political meetings were postponed because the members of Parliament were in the revival meetings. Theatrical companies quit going to Wales because no one would attend their shows. Magistrates were presented with white gloves in many towns to signify that there were *no* arrests. The prisons were emptied. Revival scenes swept the universities day after day for months. Over 70,000 names of new converts were reported in the papers in just two months.

# Chapter Ten

# They Took Up The Cross

Time constraints in the meetings were forgotten. Announced to begin a certain hour, people would gather hours before. No one knew when the services would end and clocks were completely ignored. Meetings began as soon as part of the congregation had assembled; there was no waiting for a human leader. There has possibly never been a religious movement so little indebted to the guiding minds of its leaders. When the evening meeting, which began at 7 o'clock, poured out at 3 o'clock next morning, other crowds were already preparing to get into the chapel for the early morning prayer meeting! In many towns all work ceased when the evangelists came. The factories and shops would sometimes close for days at a time so the people could attend the meetings.

A famous reporter of the great London Daily visited the meetings of the young prophet of Loughor in order to describe to the people in London the amazing scenes about which they had heard. He wrote:

> I found the flame of Welsh religious enthusiasm as smokeless as its coal. There are no advertisements, no brass bands, no posters. All the paraphernalia of the got-up job (typical meetings) are conspicuous by

their absence. There is no instrumental music. The pipe organs lie unused. There is no need of instruments for in and around and beneath surge the all-prevailing thrill and throb of a multitude praying, and singing as they pray.

The vast congregations are soberly sane, as orderly and at least as reverent as any congregation I ever saw beneath the dome of St. Paul's cathedral. Tier above tier in the crowded aisle to the loftiest gallery sit or stand as necessity dictates, eager hundreds of serious men and thoughtful women, their eyes riveted upon the platform or UPON WHATEVER PART OF THE BUILDING IS THE STORM CENTER OF THE MEETING. The vast majority of the congregation are stalwart young miners.

"We must obey the Spirit" is the watchword of Evan Roberts, and he is as obedient as the humblest of his audience. No one uses a hymn book; no one gives out a hymn. The last person to control the meeting in any way is Evan Roberts. You feel that the thousand or fifteen hundred persons before you have become merged into one myriad-headed but single-souled personality. You can watch what they call "the influence of the power of the Spirit" playing over the congregation as an ebbing wind plays over the surface of the pond.

A very remarkable instance of this abandonment of the meeting to the spontaneous impulse, not merely of those within the walls but of those crowded outside, who were unable to get in, occurred on Sunday night. Twice the order of proceeding, if order it can be called, was altered by the crowd outside who, by some mysterious impulse started a hymn on their own account which was at once taken up by the congregation within. On one of these occasions Evan Roberts was addressing the meeting. He at once gave way and the singing became general.

The meeting always breaks out into a compassionate and consoling song, until the soloist, having recovered his breath, rises from his knees and sings a song.

The praying and singing are both wonderful. But more impressive than either are the breaks which occur when utterance can be no more, and then the sobbing in the silence momentarily heard is drowned in a tempest of melody. No need for an organ. The assembly is its own organ as a thousand or fifteen hundred sorrowing or rejoicing hearts find expression in the sacred Psalmody of their native hills.

Repentance, open confession, intercessory prayer, and above all else this marvelous musical liturgy—a liturgy unwritten, but heartfelt mighty chorus' rising like the thunder of the surge of the rock-bound shore, ever and anon broken by the flute like note of the singing sisters whose melody is as sweet and as spontaneous as the music of the throstle in the grove or the martin in the skies. And all this vast quivering, throbbing, singing, praying, exultant multitude intensely conscious of the all-pervading influence of some invisible reality—now for the first time moving palpable though not tangible in their midst. They call it THE SPIRIT OF GOD.

## The Cross Was The Center

The following recorded prayer of Evan Roberts captures succinctly the central emphasis of and devotion of the revival evangelists:

Lord Jesus, help us now through the Holy Spirit to come face to face with the cross. Whatever the hindrances may be, we commit the service to Thee. Put us all under the Blood. Oh, Lord, place the Blood on all our past up to this moment. We thank Thee for the Blood. In the Name of Jesus Christ bind the devil this moment. We point to the Cross of Christ. It is our Cross and we take its conquest.

Reveal the Cross through the Name of Jesus. Oh, open the Heavens. Descend upon us now. Tear open our hearts; give us such a sight of Calvary that our hearts may be broken. Oh Lord, descend now; open our hearts to receive the heart that bled for us. If we are to be fools—make us fools for Thee. Take us, spirit, soul, and body. WE ARE THINE. Thou hast purchased us.

Reveal the Cross for the sake of Jesus—the Cross that is to conquer the world. Place us under the Blood. Forbid that we should think of what men may say of us. Oh speak—speak—speak, Lord Jesus. Thy Words are "wine indeed". Oh, reveal the Cross, beloved Jesus—the cross in its glory.

Reign in every heart for the sake of Jesus. Lord, do Thou help us to see the dying Savior. Enable us to see Him conquering the hosts of darkness. Claim victory for Thy Son, now Lord. He is worthy to have the victory. THOU ART THE ALL-POWERFUL GOD. OH, CLAIM VICTORY. We shall give all the glory to Thy Name. No one else has a right to the glory but Thee. Take it, Lord. Glorify Thy Son in this meeting. OH, HOLY SPIRIT—DO THOU WORK THROUGH US AND IN US NOW. Speak Thy Word in power for Thy Name's sake. Amen—and Amen!

The love, sufferings, death and resurrection of Jesus were the theme of every meeting, every sermon, every prayer and became the passion of every heart. The people were not being converted to a new doctrine, a denomination, a personality, or even the new movement—they were converted to Jesus. The leaders of the revival held steadfast to the exhortation of the apostle Paul, who said:

> And when I came to you, brethren, I did not come with superiority of speech or of wisdom, proclaiming to you the testimony of God.

> For I determined to know nothing among you except Jesus Christ and Him crucified.

Conversions in the Welsh Revival were not just statistics, they were new births. Men and women were so radically changed that being "born again" was not just a cliché—it was a reality. The new believer's first encounter with the Lord was not the promise of blessings, it was a profound comprehension of his own sinful condition. When moved by the Spirit to come to the wells of salvation, converts did not just raise their hands in the back of the building to acknowledge their "decision," they were racked with such a holy desperation for the mercy of the Savior that they tumbled to the floor as if in physical pain. Those under conviction would sometimes writhe in their own tears until they gained the assurance of forgiveness; then their grief would turn into a joy of an equal depth that would be impossible to contain. As the meetings began to disband, often at two or three in the morning, new converts just could not leave and would continue singing, praying and at times laughing uncontrollably until the prayer meetings started at sunrise.

# Chapter Eleven

# Can A Nation Be Born Again?

The effects of the revival on the nation of Wales are remarkable in all of history. The First and Second Great Awakenings undoubtably changed the genetic codes of Britain and America, but history simply reveals no other examples where the changes in society equaled what happened in Wales. Some of the cities and towns that had been on the brink of anarchy, with violent crimes increasing out of control, during the revival did not record a single arrest. Others would record but one or two for such crimes as drunkenness in public. Many of the jails and prisons were completely empty.

Before the revival there had been almost a plague of drunkenness and gambling. During the revival taverns were either closed or turned into meeting halls. Instead of wasting their earnings on drinking and gambling, workers started taking their wages home to their families. Because of the conviction of the Holy Spirit, restitution became a fruit of repentance and outstanding debts were being paid by thousands of young converts. These two factors alone resulted in a substantial economic impact on the whole community.

The famous Welsh singing festivals which had been so popular closed down during the revival because their famous vocalists, such as the "Sankeys" and "Alexanders" were now singing hymns in the revival meetings. The theaters and football stadiums likewise closed down for lack of interest. Political meetings were canceled or abandoned. Many of the elected officials, even those from London, abandoned their seats in parliament to participate in the revival meetings. Businesses founded upon honorable trades and products prospered. Those that traded on vice went out of business. Possibly never before in history has an entire society been so profoundly transformed by a spiritual revival in such a short time.

## How the Revival Affected The Church

The most significant result of this revival on the church was that all church prejudices and denominational barriers completely collapsed as believers and pastors of all denominations worshipped the Lord together. The quarrels of local Christians were either forgotten or instantly healed, appearing incomprehensible and petty in the light of the Lord's glory.

One outstanding characteristic of the revival was the confession of sin, and it swelled over from the unsaved to the saved, who were broken and humbled by the revelation of the cross of Christ. Bitterness and resentment seemed unthinkable as all were compelled to gaze upon the Lord's great mercy and love. This unity was not caused by persecution, but by the glory and presence of the Lord. This was a profound historic example of how all of our individual crowns will be cast to the feet of the Lamb when He enters His church.

Churches that had struggled to keep the doors open for the few saints who would attend their services were now faced with the problem of how to accommodate the multitudes that were causing even the prayer meetings to over-flow. There was not a single congregation in Wales that was really prepared for the magnitude of this revival. Some of the pastors strove to serve all of the new converts and see that they were properly incorporated into congregations, but to most the revival was "gloriously out of control."

Some of the pastors quickly burned out by trying to do too much. In fact, it is probable that the revival could have lasted much longer had the leaders paced themselves better. As Charles Finney had said, "No revival can last if the workers do not learn to rest." True revivals bring many strains upon congregations and Christian workers that few are prepared for. Almost every church or mission in the country grew dramatically, frequently doubling or even quadrupling in membership, and many maintained these members for years after the revival ended.

Even so, multitudes who were touched by the revival and had a genuine encounter with the Lord were also lost again to the world because there were not enough workers to care for them, to help to raise them spiritually. It is hard to take the time to equip other workers and ministries in the heat of revival. Had this been done before the revival it is most certain that many more of those who committed themselves to the Lord during this time could have been established in the faith and truly added to the church.

## The Fire Spreads

A true revival cannot be kept local. Revival is like a fire that is carried by the wind—its sparks will ignite the dry wood and grass in every direction that it blows. Sparks can be carried by letters, phone calls or newspapers—but most of all they are carried by people. Localities that were far removed from the center of the Welsh Revival, broke out into revival just at the news of what was happening in Wales. In many of these places the awakening seemed to be just as intense as what was going on in Wales, but it is probable that the spiritual temperature of the entire world was raised a few degrees by this great outpouring of the Spirit.

On April 8, 1905, nearly ten thousand miles away in Los Angeles, California, a young man named Frank Bartleman heard F.B. Meyer preach. As he described the revival that was going on in Wales and his meeting with Evan Roberts, Bartleman later wrote: "My soul was stirred to the depths, having read of this revival shortly before. I then and there promised God He should have full right of way with me; if He could use me" (*Another Wave of Revival*, Frank Bartleman, p. 8).

Later Bartleman, James Seymore and Pastor Smale read the books *The Great Revival In Wales*, by S.B. Shaw and G. Campbell Morgan's tract *The Revival In Wales* and were stirred to earnestly seek the Lord for revival in Los Angeles. In May they were sent 5,000 pamphlets titled *The Revival in Wales*, which they distributed in the churches. Several letters were then exchanged with Evan Roberts himself. Shortly thereafter the Azusa Street Revival erupted into the great Pentecostal Revival that was to directly impact hundreds of millions of lives and continues to burn to this day.

Bartleman, Seymore and Smale were unknowns ministering in a tiny little unknown mission on a side street in Los Angeles. Evan Roberts could not have known the impending spiritual destiny of these men. Because he took the time to communicate with such unknowns, history was changed and the last day course of the church was set on its course. These three great spiritual pioneers continually referred to their encouragement from Evan Roberts as they pursued the fullness of God's Spirit in their lives.

## He Is Still Born In Stables

In Biblical times the stable was a most offensive place. The floors were composed of decades worth of impacted dung and other filth. The stench was so great they were placed as far away from other dwellings as possible. By today's standards, they would not even be fit for animals. That the Lord of Glory would choose such a place to make His entry into this world is one of the more profound revelations of His message to man. We would do well not to miss His point as He has not stopped using such places to make His appearances. Just as the Lord chose Wales, the least of the principalities of the British Isles, He later chose the tiny little Azusa Street mission and three humble, but courageous black pastors to change the face of modern Christianity.

Human reasoning would never lead us to a stable to find God. The only way He could be found was by revelation; only those who were led by the Spirit would come. This has not changed. That which has been born of God is usually repulsive to the pride and presumptions of men. The Lord has never birthed a true revival out of the great theological centers and bastions of influence. **"God resists the proud and gives His grace to the humble"** (James 4:6). The more humble we are the more grace we can receive.

After His birth, Jesus was then raised in the most despised town in the most despised nation of Israel. Even His physical appearance was such that no one would be attracted to Him (Isaiah 53:2). He then left this world after the most degrading torture and execution yet devised by the base and demented schemes of fallen men. This gospel is foolishness to the natural man, and it always will be. It will never attract those who live by human wisdom or those who are attracted by the pride of political influence. Only those who love truth more than anything else in this world will walk with Him in the reproach of the true gospel.

The birth, life and death of Jesus put the ax to the root of the tree of human wisdom and pride—the fruit of the Tree of Knowledge of Good and Evil. It is the most powerful message the creation has ever heard; it is the most profound testimony of the character and nature of God. When we embellish this gospel to make it appeal to carnal men, we destroy its power to set them free, and we ourselves begin to drift from the path of life. For this reason Paul preached nothing but Christ and Him crucified. He knew that if men were to come by any other message their conversions would be false.

To see what the Lord is doing we may have to go to places that require the death of our flesh and sometimes our reputations. We must have the heart of Simeon and Anna, who could see in a mere infant the salvation of the world. Don't be discouraged if the fruit is not yet apparent; look for the seed that will become the fruit. This does not mean that He is found only in the poor, the wretched and the despised, but that is where He is usually found. **"But God has chosen the foolish things of the world to shame the wise, and God has chosen the weak things of the world to shame the things which are strong" (I Corinthians 1:27)**

The true gospel will never appeal to the carnal nature of man—it will confront that nature and put the ax to its root. As the apostle declared, **"If I were still trying to please men, I would not be a bond-servant of Christ (Galatians 1:10).** We must choose who we are going to please. It will be Christ or man, but it will never be both. If we are not willing to embrace that which appears foolish to the worldly wise, we will not embrace that which God is doing. Again the church is facing a radical choice—will we preach a gospel that appeals to men while leaving their souls in jeopardy? Or will we preach the gospel that will change the heart and save the soul of those who will humble themselves to receive it. Both in Wales and at Azusa Street they chose God, and the whole world has benefitted from their choice.

## Sparks Fly

The Welsh Revival had a powerful impact on many other unexpected places. Visiting preachers and ordinary believers who had come to see the "burning bush" returned home to start fires in their own churches, mission fields, and cities. Christians all over the world became encouraged at the news, and nothing ignites evangelism like encouragement in the church. When Christians are encouraged in their faith they cannot help but to share the hope that is within them.

Only the Lord could know how many souls were birthed into the kingdom by the fires started in Wales, by that handful of young, zealous believers who yearned for Him, opened the door for Him, and then followed Him.

The Welsh-speaking colonies in America and elsewhere were quickly set ablaze with revival. India was swept with the fire. All of Britain was touched and the Continent was invaded by wave after wave of evangelists, pastors, Bible teachers, and even new believers who could not sit still with the good news that was burning inside of them. In Scandinavia there are still hundreds of churches that trace their birth to the Welsh Revival. Rees Howells, the great intercessor was among the young evangelists who carried the fire from Wales to the mission field. Waves of evangelists and missionaries swept across the continents of Africa and Asia, saving souls and planting churches, Bible schools and colleges to the ends of the earth.

A young Latvian student from Spurgeon's College in London left his classes on hearing of the fire of God in Wales and headed for Swansea. There the Spirit of God came upon him so mightily that when he returned to his native Russia the revival broke out there. Over thirty years later this man testified that he was still conscious of the effect of the Welsh revival upon his ministry, which resulted directly in tens of thousands coming to Christ and in building some two hundred churches in Eastern Europe. It is probable that similar testimonies could be given from men of God in almost every nation on earth. The fire was obviously centered in Wales, but the warmth of it filled the earth.

Pastors D.P. and W.J. Williams, founders of the Apostolic Church in Europe, were both converted during the Welsh Revival. These men carried the fire of their conversions until their deaths. They impacted much of the church in Europe and started a worldwide movement devoted to returning to apostolic church government that continues today. It is impossible to speculate about what the twentieth century church would have been like without the extraordinary impact of the Welsh Revival. Though some denominations would not even acknowledge that the Welsh Revival was from God, it is probable that every church, movement and denomination was influenced and changed to some degree by this mighty outburst of God, upon such a lowly and needy people.

# PART II

# Lessons From The Welsh Revival

# Chapter Twelve

# Why The Fire Falls

The first and most obvious question that researchers tend to ask about the Welsh Revival is: Why did the Lord do it there? James E. Stewart concluded simply that God sends His fire where it is likely to catch and spread, that "Wales provided the necessary tinder." This is at least a part of the reason. But this leads us to another obvious question: *What is the necessary tinder?*

*Tinder is wood that is dry enough to burn easily.* Both the Scriptures and history testify that *a holy desperation precedes new beginnings.* The Lord waited for Israel to get so desperate in her bondage to the Egyptians that she would cry out to Him for help. From then the history of Israel is a repetitious cycle of their becoming complacent when blessed, which led to backsliding, which led to bondage, which led to a desperate repentance and calling out to God, which led to deliverance and then blessing again. This cycle continues through church history as well. It seems that the church will only seek the Lord so as to find Him when she is utterly desperate; only the thirsty seek after water, only the hungry seek after food.

A call to break this cycle is given in the Lord's words to the Laodicean church. His words to the seven churches in Revelation address possibly every phase of church growth and development. The Laodicean church seems to personify the prosperous, comfortable and lukewarm churches that can probably be found somewhere in the world at any given time. The Lord's rebuke to the church in this condition is terrible, but His promises to those who overcome this condition are the greatest promises given to any of the churches! They are to dine with Him and to sit with Him *on His throne!* This is in contrast to the great company of chapter seven that stands "before the throne." These promises speak of receiving the very best spiritual food, and attaining the very highest position of power and authority.

Because the Laodicean church seems to so accurately reflect the church in the West at the present time, many who walk in the intensity of the mission fields, or in the persecuted church, have written off the church in the West as having any spiritual relevance for this time. Actually the opposite has been true. The Lord's call to the church in Laodicea was to **"be *zealous* therefore, and repent"** (Revelation 3:19b). Those who have been able to overcome the lukewarm spirit in the West, and pursue the Lord with **zeal**, have been rewarded with almost unprecedented teaching and spiritual authority, which has been used to bless the church world-wide.

This is to say that to be in a hard, dry place spiritually can definitely help people to seek the Lord, but there are some who will seek Him just as zealously even when things are going very well. Many are crying for economic judgment to come upon the West to help bring revival, and it may come to that, but why wait for it? For many this is nothing more than an excuse for not preaching the gospel now. Actually, both the Scriptures and history testify that men are more inclined to curse God in times of economic collapse than to seek Him. Most of the great revivals in history came *before* the judgment, not during or after.

## Revival Precedes Judgment

There is no more devastating judgment than war. The first "Great Awakening" in America preceded the Revolutionary War, which terribly devastated the cities and countryside of America. The "Second Great Awakening" preceded the Civil War, which was the most devastating war in America's history. The Welsh Revival, which greatly impacted the whole world, but especially Europe, preceded World War I.

Germany during the 1930's is a good example of the tendency of men during times of great economic collapse—they are more likely to turn to the tyranny of a strong dictator than to the Lord. Thinking that it will take economic judgment to bring revival to the West is evidence that the gospel now preached in the West has been very subtly changed from the Lord coming to save people from their sins to Him coming to save us from our troubles.

Nowhere in Scripture does it say that circumstances will lead men to Christ. None of those that the Lord Himself called when He walked the earth seemed to be in a place of personal desperation. The Holy Spirit was not sent to create circumstances to lead men to Christ, but to convict the world of sin—which alone will properly lead men to the Savior.

Wales was never a very wealthy region, but during the time of the Welsh Revival, the whole world was in a time of relative economic prosperity, and so was Wales. They were in a time of gross moral debauchery, but "where sin abounds, grace much more abounds." The world is now finding itself in a similar time of relative economic prosperity, but are pressing the outer limits on moral corruption. The world is NOW ripe for revival! We do not need circumstances to help us—we need the Holy Spirit to "convict the world of sin," which always leads to Jesus, who came to "save us from our sins."

## The Beginning

It is hard to trace the exact beginning of the Welsh Revival because those who were close to it counted the experience too sacred to be revealed publicly. Every significant outpouring of the Spirit seems to have been preceded by earnest, agonizing, intercession, accompanied by a heart-brokenness and humiliation before God. Pastors and their flocks were deeply concerned about the terrible discrepancy between the heart-stirring record in the Book of Acts and their present condition. This yearning to see the Lord move again did seem to prevail throughout Wales before the month of November, 1904. The Holy Spirit began convicting the church of her sin of lukewarmness before He began convicting the heathen of their sin. This was a gradual work that obviously evolved over many years. As Stewart observed:

> "It is improbable that this revival or any other is of sudden origin. When the revival manifests itself in a mighty way it comes suddenly as in the days of Hezekiah, but even so, its origins begin with the Holy Spirit of God moving effectively in individual lives in private. Let no one pray for revival—let no one pray for a mighty baptism of power who is not prepared for deep heart-searchings and confession of sin in his personal life. Revival, in its beginnings, is a most humiliating experience. When one, like Isaiah, sees himself in the light of God's holiness he must inevitably cry, 'Woe is me!'".

## The Ultimate Spiritual Desperation

Deep spiritual awakenings, whether in local churches or in whole countries, begin with desperate people. Hannah, the prophet Samuel's mother, is a good example of those whom God uses to give birth to His purposes. Hannah became so desperate for a son that she was willing to give that son back to the Lord after she received him. This kind of devotion never fails to move the Lord to respond to His people, and it is what He must see in His people before He can trust them with true revival. When we are willing to give everything that is born back to Him, for His glory, releasing control of it for Him to raise it as He sees fit, we are then ready.

The Lord has proven over and over that He will answer the prayers of desperate Christians, Christians who are sick of the tired, weary, cold, mechanical "services," who are heartbroken over the deadness of the church, over sinners who are eternally lost, and who are desperate about their own spiritual condition. While it is true that when the awakening does come there is "joy unspeakable and full of glory," this never seems to be the case during the days preceding revival. There must be days of no song before the songs of the Holy Spirit come, groans and mourning before the joy and laughter. And always there must be that devotion of Hannah to give what is born back to God.

It may be for this reason that those who are on the forefront of the previous move of God are seldom used to ignite the next move of God. It is possible that those who are used to lead two succeeding spiritual movements will be the very first in history to do so. It appears that those who have been a part of the most recent moves of God still have enough of the lingering blessings that they are not compelled to continue seeking the Lord with the holy desperation that seems to be a prerequisite for revival.

## Pride—The Death of Spiritual Advancement

It has been almost universal that those who are mightily used by God begin to feel at least a subtle pride in it. Therefore, many of those who were mightily used by Him in the past are actually being resisted by Him when the time for the next movement begins. This pride has often manifested itself by those involved declaring themselves to be the last move of God before the Lord returns. This delusion prohibits any further receiving from the Lord. How could another, succeeding movement be from God if they were the last? Such presumption destroys our ability to continue moving with the cloud of God's presence. For this reason it seems that the Holy Spirit still has to find those who are "formless and void" before He can move again in a creative way.

I would also emphasize that this seems to be required before He can move in a *creative way*. The fact is, almost every move of God is, in some ways, profoundly different from the previous ways that He has moved. There are, of course, some general principles that could be applied to most revivals or awakenings, but true revivals often include many tradition busting acts of the Holy Spirit that are completely new to those involved. The God who makes every snowflake different obviously delights in diversity. If there is a single common denominator to every revival or spiritual advance, it would be that they all have profound differences. The nature of the Creator is to be creative!

## Summary

Historically, we can find almost every kind of moral and economic condition in which the Lord has originated some form of revival. Men are still in a fallen, sinful state and need Christ regardless of their circumstances. The only condition that the Lord seems to require before sending a revival or awakening, is that His people ask, seek and knock until He opens the windows of heaven.

The world is in sin and in desperate need of the Savior— now! Repeatedly the Scriptures warn—**"TODAY, if you would hear His voice, do not harden your hearts" (Psalm 95:7, Hebrews 3:7,15, 4:7).** We do not need to be looking at human conditions when seeking or praying for revival—we need to seek the heart of God—TODAY, for what He will do TODAY. We must not be like the cripple sitting by the pool waiting for someone to stir the waters when the King Himself is standing right next to us.

Many people are waiting for their neighbors, family or friends to come to a place of desperation before they will witness to them. They do not need desperation—they need the Holy Spirit. They do not need to be desperate because of their circumstances to come to Jesus—they need to be desperate *because of their sin.* If we would shake ourselves from our lukewarmness and do what we can TODAY to witness for Jesus, the whole world would TODAY be experiencing a revival even greater than Wales. This will happen. Why not TODAY? As Paul instructed Timothy, we should:

> **Preach the word; be ready in season and out of season; reprove, rebuke, exhort, with great patience and instruction (II Timothy 4:2).**

As Peter also made a remarkable exhortation: **But the day of the Lord will come like a thief... what sort of people ought you to be in holy conduct and godliness,** *looking for and hastening* **the coming of the day of God... (II Peter 3:10-12).** Has it ever occurred to you that we can actually "hasten the coming of the day of God?" We can!

# Chapter Thirteen

# Renewal vs. Restoration

This is one of the major controversies that seems to rise during every revival or awakening: Does the Lord want this revival to renew the present church structure, or give birth to a whole new structure, usually known as "restoration?" It is obvious that He wants to do both! However, those who are committed to renewal are usually blind to His purposes for restoration. Likewise, those who are committed to a theology of restoration are usually blind to His purposes in renewal. This blindness on the part of each usually works to short circuit and bring to a premature end many true moves of God.

Some do not believe that men's shortcomings can stop a true move of God, but He does require that certain conditions be met and maintained within His church if He is to visit with His manifest presence. One of these primary conditions is unity. A study of all the enemy's schemes to thwart the advancement of God's purposes exposes his strategy to create division in the church. The devil seems to understand that a house divided cannot stand. One of the primary controversies that he uses to thwart revivals or movements concerns the conflict between renewal and restoration theology.

Failure to understand God's purposes for both renewal and restoration often keeps the leaders of one revival, or movement from being used in a subsequent one. Few things will breathe more life into a mature, established, but lukewarm congregation like a wave of new converts. The Lord uses new converts to help renew and keep the faith fresh in more mature believers. In this same way the Lord uses new movements that plant new churches to help keep the faith of the entire church fresh and seeking more of Him.

Only those who are subject to the spirit of territorial preservation are threatened by new churches in their area. Those who have a vision for the kingdom of God, and not just their own kingdoms, will not only welcome new churches, but will pray for them and seek to help them in any way that they can. Just as the high priest carried the stones of all of the tribes on his breastplate, those who walk in the highest callings carry all of God's people on their hearts, regardless of which "tribe" (i.e. denomination or movement) they come from.

## The Problem Of Time

When we look back at some of the great revivalists and reformers in history, it seems as if their ministries spanned great periods of time, but in fact the opposite is true. Few of even the greatest leaders in church history sustained the peak time of their leadership for more than a few years. They may have lived on past the time of their greatest anointing, and they may have maintained some influence, but their true time of leadership—when they carried the church forward— was usually brief. This period was sometimes less than a year, and rarely more than five years.

Unfortunately, it is a fact of church history that new movements that truly are "new wineskins" become "old wineskins" much faster than we would like to think. To date, it does not seem that this trend has been avoided by a single movement. Can a new wineskin remain new, or is it inevitable that they each become old, brittle and unable to contain the new wine?

Through studying the "wineskin principle" I have become convinced that the Lord must usually find a new wineskin for each new movement, or advance for His purposes. However, it is also true that, in Biblical times, there was a process for renewing old wineskins by soaking them in oil and then water. Recent moves of the Holy Spirit indicate that the Lord is both bringing forth new wineskins, and renewing old ones. There does not have to be a conflict between the doctrines of renewal and restoration. It is obvious that the Lord is doing both. That is why the apostle Paul, on his missionary journeys, would always visit synagogues, seeking their renewal, *and* plant new churches.

## The Dry Bones Principle

It seems that many of those involved in the present, cutting edge moves of God are unable to accept God's devotion to renewing denominations, or previous movements. Likewise, those who have been a part of the most recent movement have such a residual blessing from it that they usually do not remain desperate enough to seek the Lord for more, and reject future movements. Those that experience a genuine renewal of the Holy Spirit are often the older denominations or movements that are so rigid and seemingly dead in their traditions that they would seem to be the most unlikely candidates for it. However, it is this very condition that makes them desperate enough to seek the Lord so as to find Him. It does seem that "the bones" of Ezekial's vision (Ezekial 37) must be *very* dry before life can be prophesied to them.

Running parallel to most movements of renewal in the church there is usually a "restoration" movement. These movements are called "restoration" because their focus is the recovering of forgotten Biblical truths. No honest student of church history could deny that this has been a driving force in church history since the Reformation, and has created significant spiritual advances. Contrary to the usual accusations about new movements being founded on "new truths," with the inference being nonbiblical truths, each true restoration movement has recovered forgotten *Biblical* truths. Those who make the accusation that restoration movements are seeking new truths are by this inherently stating that they have all of the truth that there is to be recovered from the Scriptures—a most deadly presumption if we are to keep from becoming an old, rigid and inflexible wineskin.

Likewise, those who are a part of new movements who begin to scorn or attack the previous movements, or their remnants, are by this exuding a pride which God Himself has declared that he will resist, which stops the movement! God really is bringing forth from His treasures things both old and new, but only the wisest of men have been able to see it, or to become a part of both. The conflict arising between these two, parallel moves of God will bring a quick halt to His grace upon each.

Unrighteous judgment, which is to judge by any other perspective but God's, is the result of either pride or fear, both of which will bring a stop to spiritual advancement. The apostle Paul exhorted his converts both to hold fast the traditions that were delivered to them and to vehemently resist the traditions that would bind them. There are some traditions that add life to the church and help to keep her on course. There are also some that can be used to supplant true spiritual life and the place of the Holy Spirit in the church.

Every revival, awakening, or movement is destined to fight a life and death battle to properly relate to tradition, while remaining open to the new thing that the Lord is doing. Those who try to utterly cast off tradition inevitably become like a train without tracks—they may have a great deal of energy and put out a lot of steam, but they will not get very far. Those who try to fall back completely on tradition are like tracks without a train—they may really lead somewhere, but they are lacking what it takes to actually get there.

For almost two years the Welsh Revival seemed to keep a wonderful balance between the new and the old. The old came to life because it was properly esteemed and received, which enabled it to be a more solid foundation from which the new could spring. This was because there was such an anointing that everyone could easily recognize just what God was doing. Sometimes the Lord anointed new songs and sometimes old ones. At times He would anoint a traditional form of service, and sometimes it was not anointed and was quickly abandoned. The trouble seems to have begun when the new form of worship that was born out of the revival became "the form" to the point of resisting occasionally going back to the old, or being open to something even newer.

## Baptized By Those Who Prepare The Way

How the new relates to the old, and vice versa, is one of the ultimate issues as to whether revival can be born, or continue once it has begun. When Jesus was asked by what authority He did His works, He pointed to the baptism of John, and asked His inquisitors whether it was of God or men. The Lord was not trying to deflect their question about the source of His authority—the answer to that question was the answer to their question.

John the Baptist was the last of the old order. That order had prepared the way from the beginning, and they had all prophesied of Jesus. John was there as the representative of that order to point to Jesus and declare that He was indeed the One of which they had all spoken. Like no other prophet or emissary from God in history, Jesus had credentials—He had been spoken of from the beginning.

Jesus did not point to the old order and declare that it was dead, a thing of the past—He honored it, and even submitted Himself to it. Jesus was connected to the past moves of God; He had His roots in them; He not only pointed to them as His credentials, He drew much of His sustenance from them, establishing His teaching by "it is written." We must do the same if we are going to walk in divine authority.

## Orthodoxy vs. The Scriptures

There can be major differences between what is considered orthodox Christianity and true Biblical Christianity. Because of this "orthodoxy" is at best a weak and impotent argument for declaring a ministry or teaching true or false. To use this argument there must be an in-depth explanation of whose perspective of orthodoxy is to be used. Catholic orthodoxy certainly is not the same as Protestant, and Baptist or Pentecostal is not the same as Protestant. However, for matters that are not clear in the Scriptures, this argument could, and should, have some weight within the particular stream or denomination involved.

The spiritual progress that has been made over the last 500 years to recover Biblical truth would have been stymied if there were not those who had the courage to reach beyond orthodoxy to stand upon the truth that is revealed in Scripture. However, the spirit in which this is done will determine whether this will actually result in a further spiritual advance in the recovery of Biblical truth, or just another sect, or heresy.

The spiritual generation gaps that have formed between subsequent movements have often caused so much discord in the Body of Christ that the potential blessing from the recovered truth is nullified by the disunity and conflict. However, this will not continue. The last statement from the Old Testament, which pointed to the New Testament, promised something different:

> **Behold, I am going to send you Elijah the prophet before the coming of the great and terrible day of the Lord.**

> **And he will restore the hearts of the fathers to their children, and the hearts of the children to their fathers, lest I come and smite the land with a curse.**

The spirit of Elijah was upon John the Baptist to prepare the way for the Lord, and the spirit of Elijah will be upon the church at the end of the age to prepare for His second coming. The true spirit of Elijah turns the hearts of the fathers to the children, and the hearts of the children to the fathers. Before the day of the Lord, before the harvest that is the end of the age, this spiritual generation gap will have been healed. The new will be properly joined to the old. The fathers will prepare the way for their spiritual sons, and the sons will properly esteem their fathers. When this unity is achieved, we will be ready for the Lord to return.

# Chapter Fourteen

# Can Intercession Bring Revival?

The intercessory ministry of the church before the Welsh Revival was extraordinary. Thousands of believers, often unknown to each other, in small towns and in the cities, cried to God day after day for the fire of revival to fall.

These prayers were not merely "a little talk with Jesus," but daily, agonizing intercession. These were devoted saints who had given their lives to the sacrifice of prayer and worship. They were so jealous for the name of God that they took personally the way Satan was being glorified all around them. Throughout the church in Wales a special yearning to see the Lord's name lifted up there was growing. The Lord was constantly reminded of what He had done in 1859, the previous period of revival in Wales that had been connected to the Second Great Awakening in America, and they begged Him to pour out His Spirit again.

Evan Roberts captured the spirit of the whole revival with the theme: BEND THE CHURCH AND SAVE THE WORLD. James E. Stewart claimed that this is the secret of every true awakening. Christians must humble themselves and get right with God so that the Spirit can break through in converting power upon the unsaved. There must be no hypocrisy; the Christian must BEND to the will of God for His life before the Spirit of God is released. When we are bent to the will of God we will be intercessors, because He "ever lives to intercede" for His people, and if we are abiding in Him we will do the same.

One of the oldest, unanswered questions about revival concerns the degree to which intercession is required to bring it to pass. It does seem that no great revival has ever taken place without there first being heaven-rending prayer on behalf of the lost and the condition of the church. But we must also ask the question: Did the intercession bring forth the revival or did the impending revival bring forth the intercession? In other words; does the travail cause the baby or does the baby cause the travail? Obviously it is the latter.

## False Spiritual Pregnancies

This is an important question because many dear saints have expended much of their lives in spiritual travail never to see a spiritual birth. In the natural there is such a thing as a false pregnancy. It is possible for a woman who wants a baby badly enough to start having the symptoms of being pregnant, even gaining weight and carrying it like a baby, when there has been no conception. Likewise, many well meaning saints have spent much of their lives in travail for revival with no fruit.

This is not to conclude that their prayer is utterly wasted, but true, effective prayer begins with discerning the heart and purposes of God, not just deciding that we want something, even something as noble as revival. There is abundant evidence that travailing intercession does precede revival, but just as a woman cannot just decide that she is going to be pregnant, it is also obvious that this is a work that the Lord must initiate. Without conception, a woman can go through endless travail, but there still is not going to be a baby. Neither can we just decide to bring forth revival.

Romans 10:6 states: **"But the righteousness based on faith speaks thus, 'Do not say in your heart, 'who will ascend into heaven?' (that is, to bring Christ down), or 'who will descend into the abyss?' (that is, to bring Christ up from the dead)."** We cannot call God down or bring Him up as mediums try to do with their incantations to demons. The Lord is not at our disposal, we are at His. True spiritual travail comes from being united with Him, just as a woman becomes pregnant through union with her husband.

Genuine spiritual travail comes as a result of spiritual conception; it is not just something that we can decide to enter into. However, when a spiritual birth is impending, we cannot keep from entering into travail, just as a woman who is about to give birth cannot just decide not to be pregnant anymore—a woman who *is* pregnant cannot just decide that she is not pregnant—there is a baby in her that *is* going to be born!

The whole world is in desperate need of revival, and before the end of this age there is going to be one so awesome and universal of which all of these other great revivals will have been just a foretaste. Even so, before we begin to agonize in prayer for it, we must be so joined to the Lord that we are impregnated with His purposes. Our intercession must be for intimacy with Him, and then with Him for His purposes.

## Keeping Our First Love

Our first love must be for the Lord, Himself, and then for His purposes. People can want revival for many different reasons, some of them selfish. Parents who love each other more than they love their children will love their children more than other parents do. If we will love the Lord more than we love His purposes, we will then be able to love His purposes properly without making them idols.

Count Ludwig von Zinzendorf was the true father of modern missions (When William Carey was called "the father of modern missions," he referred to Zinzendorf and the Moravians as his inspiration and the true heirs of this title). When the ship carrying the first two Moravian missionaries sent to the West Indies was pulling away from the dock, the former fiancé of one of them cried to her departing love that she would probably never see again, "Why? Why would you do something like this? He replied simply, "So that the Savior will receive the reward of His sacrifice." True evangelism and true revival is born out of a love for the Lord, not just a love for the lost, though that is of course important.

True intercession is likewise founded upon a desire to be united with the Lord, not just an effort to get Him to do something. Intercession is born out of maintaining the posture of John at the last supper—of leaning our head upon His breast where we can feel His heartbeat. There our hearts will start to beat in unison with His, and that which is on His heart will be what is on our hearts. This is what it really means to pray to the Father in the Lord's name. Praying in the "name of Jesus" is not just using the word "Jesus," but it is praying with His authority.

## To Change The Lord's Mind

However, there are Scriptural examples where intercession was used to *change* the Lord's mind or intended actions. One of the most prominent examples is when the Lord had determined to destroy Israel and Moses interceded to change His mind (see Exodus 32:11-14). Certainly this is the prerogative that a wife would have with her husband, and the church has this as His bride.

Even so, we can see in this example that the intercession was made on behalf of the Lord's interests, as Moses was concerned that the reputation of the Lord would be that He could bring the people out of Egypt but He could not bring them into the Promised Land. When Peter tried to intercede with the Lord to prevent Him from going to Calvary, the Lord rebuked him by calling him Satan, saying **"... you are not setting your mind on God's interests, but man's" (Matthew 16:23).** Fallen man's interests are in conflict with God's purposes, including His purposes for fallen man. To be able to intercede properly for men we must do so from God's perspective, by His Spirit.

## Summary

Intercession is one of the most important functions of the church—the church is called to be "a house of prayer for all peoples." However, we must be sure that we are praying in harmony with God's purposes and not just for what we think we need.

Elijah was obviously in touch with God and he actually prayed *for* judgment to come upon his nation. It was the judgment of God that brought the repentance which brought the revival in his time. We may want to pray earnestly for revival but what is really needed is judgment, and vice versa. Prayer is not used to change the mind of the Lord as much as it is used to bring us into one mind with Him. His ways are higher than our ways and His thoughts are higher than our thoughts. One of the purposes for intercession is to bring us into harmony with Him and what He is doing.

Does this mean that we just should not pray at all until we are sure of what His will is? No. Many would never pray because they never are sure of such things. What righteous father who knew that his daughter was trying to do his will, even though she may not have understood it properly and therefore made a mistake, would be upset with his daughter? The Lord is pleased that we try, even if we do not do it properly.

A good example of this is when Martha and Mary came out to meet Jesus after their brother Lazarus had died. Martha came out first to meet him and said, **"Lord, if you had been here my brother would not have died" (John 11:21)** When Jesus told her that her brother would rise, she said that she knew he would rise again on the last day. Again the Lord corrected her by saying, **"I am the resurrection..." (verse 25).** Then Mary came out and made the same wrong declaration, **"Lord, if you had been here, my brother would**

**not have died" (verse 32).** Martha had provoked the Lord to give her a good teaching about the resurrection, but when Mary came out and made the same wrong statement, His reaction was different: **When Jesus therefore saw her weeping... He was deeply moved in spirit, and was troubled... Jesus wept" (verses 33,35).**

Mary was just as wrong in her discernment of the presence and power of Jesus as her sister had been. Martha was devoted to serving the Lord and Mary was one of His best friends, but Mary had given herself to "the best part," sitting at His feet and just being close to Him. Martha could move the Lord to give her a great teaching, but Mary could actually, even when she was wrong, *move God deeply in spirit*, and *cause God to weep!* The Lord is not nearly as uptight and religious as we tend to be. He is moved far more by relationship than by proper procedure. We should want to do things properly and in order, but we must first of all understand that He is our loving Father who wants more than anything to be close to us.

After Peter had the great revelation that Jesus was the Messiah, the Son of God, he was given the keys to the kingdom. Peter's very next words prompted Jesus to call him "Satan." But even though he made such a terrible mistake the Lord did not take those keys away from him. In fact, it seems that one of the main ingredients of the Lord's own discipleship program was to create an environment where his men could make mistakes, and learn from them. Peter made great mistakes, but he also had great victories. He walked on the water, if for only a brief time, but it was more than anyone else had done. He would deny the Lord, but then he would stand up on the Day of Pentecost and use the keys he had been given.

If we are going to make mistakes, let us make them on the side of trying to do His will. Let us seek to know His will when we pray, understanding that almost everything He requires us to do is by faith, which means we will seldom be absolutely sure. If we are seeking to know His will we will become increasingly knowledgeable of His ways, we will pray more and more according to His will, and we will learn much from our mistakes, as well as our unanswered prayers. One of the most important prayers that we might now utter is "Lord, teach us to pray."

# Chapter Fifteen

# Idealism vs. Revelation

There is a difference between idealism and revelation. Idealism, even spiritual idealism, is a subtle form of humanism and is a manifestation of human pride. Revelation comes from God, but idealism has its origin with man. Even in its best form, idealism is still rooted in the tree of the knowledge of good and evil.

It seems probable that Jessie Penn-Lewis played a significant part in bringing the great Welsh Revival to a premature end, even though she seemed to have had the best of intentions. The reports were that she persuaded Evan Roberts to withdraw from the revival because she thought he was getting too much of the attention that should have gone only to the Lord.

As is the case with many great leaders, their strengths can also be their weaknesses. The thought that he may be getting some of the attention that belonged to his beloved Lord appalled Evan Roberts. He followed Jesse Penn-Lewis' advice and withdrew. When he did the revival quickly died.

The idealistic would contend that if it had been a true revival then removing any man would not have made a difference. The entire testimony of both Scripture and history testifies differently. Because the Lord entrusted the authority of this earth to men, He always looks for men to stand in the gap when He wants to move on the earth. True revival can only be ignited by God, but God will always move through men.

There must be the human side of revival; it was to be "The sword of the Lord —*and Gideon.*" Many, seeking to duplicate historic revivals, have tried to remove human initiative completely so that what will happen will be solely of the Holy Spirit. But the Spirit does not work except through men. The Lord always uses chosen vessels for His work. Evan Roberts is a classic study of the type of vessel He can use. Like John the Baptist, he was given to preparing the way for the Lord, pointing to Him, and being willing to decrease as He increased. However, it was important that John not decrease until the Lord increased. This is the point that many seeking revival miss.

John had to increase before he could decrease. The Lord gave John such an anointing that an entire nation was stirred. It was only after he had the nation's attention that he pointed to the One who was greater. John had to allow the Lord to raise him up and give him the attention of the people or he would not have been able to accomplish his purpose. It is true that many who reach this point prove unwilling to decrease as the Lord increases, but that does not negate the principle. Many more never get to the place where they can point to the Lord and testify of Him because they are unwilling to be elevated to a place where this is possible.

It has been God's purpose from the beginning to use men to do His work. The Lord planted the garden but he put man in it to cultivate it and keep it. No farmer has ever grown corn; he plants it and cultivates it but only God can cause the corn to grow. But neither has God ever planted a perfect field of corn without using a man. Of course the Lord could do it Himself but He has chosen to work through men to accomplish His purposes on this earth. To be greatly used by God is not to steal His glory, but to show it forth in a greater way, as long as we keep pointing to Him.

It is often a religious spirit, which is an evil spirit, that seeks to deny man that union with God in His work, usually with idealistic delusions of man getting too much of the glory. It is right to acknowledge that man is but the "earthen vessel" and that the glory is all God's, but it is humanistic idealism that, in a sense, denies that the glory of the Lord should be in an earthen vessel at all.

It would be unfair to indict Jessie Penn-Lewis for single handedly stopping the Welsh Revival, even though many of Evan Roberts' friends and co-workers in the revival did just that. Evan Roberts left the work and went to live in the Penn-Lewis home where he effectively became a spiritual hermit, never again being used in ministry.

Years later, Roberts and Penn-Lewis co-authored a book entitled *War On The Saints* that was used to condemn the emerging Pentecostal revival as "the work of an invading host of evil spirits." Penn-Lewis had reacted strongly during the Welsh Revival to the Pentecostal demonstrations, and this book seemed to be a reaction to her dislike of their overly emotional influence. Later editions of *War On The Saints* were edited by the publishers to remove the extreme and offensive attacks on Pentecostals, but it still contains, in my opinion, a general tenor that can hinder the believer's ability to move in the gifts of the Spirit. Penn-Lewis' position is stated by J.C. Metcalfe, who wrote the forward to the book (*War On The Saints*, Christian Literature Crusade, pp. viii):

> An aftermath of the Welsh Revival at the dawn of the present century was the rise of a number of extreme cults, often stressing a return to "pentecostal" practices. Mrs. Penn-Lewis, who had witnessed much of the Revival as the representative of The Life Of Faith, saw clearly the peril of these fanatical teachings, and in collaboration with Mr. Evan Roberts, who played so prominent a part in the Revival, wrote a book, *War On The Saints*. In this book these extreme and overbalanced beliefs and practices are categorically branded as the work of an invading host of evil

spirits. The word "deception" might be said to be the key word of the book—a term which is in complete harmony with the findings both of John Wesley and Dr. Henson.

A sincere jealousy for God to receive the glory that is due Him permeates Jessie Penn-Lewis' books, and they do contain many sound principles, but much of her teaching is both reactionary and sown with idealism. Many of Evan Roberts closest friends and associates denied that *War On The Saints* was a true reflection of the Evan Roberts they had known. They testified that the book was contrary to the spirit of the revival, and decried the fact that Evan would no longer relate to the body of Christ or even see his own family again after moving in with the Penn-Lewis family.

Historically criticism has proven to be one of the enemy's foremost weapons to stop revival. When Paul and Barnabas healed the cripple in Lystra, the people were so impressed that they actually wanted to worship them. After restraining them, a few Jews come down from Antioch and Iconium with no power, just criticism, and the same crowd that had wanted to worship the apostles then stoned them! Critics are the enemy's most effective agents in either stopping or at least side-tracking the work of the Lord.

Jessie Penn-Lewis may be one of the classic historic examples of how heresy hunting or idealism can be used by the enemy to derail true works of the Holy Spirit. Some teaching imparts more faith in the enemy to deceive than faith in the Holy Spirit to lead us into all truth. Others, with a spirit of human idealism, seek to turn people from anything but the New Jerusalem, which has not yet descended. New movements will be immature, and they will make some mistakes. Unfortunately many of those who are always looking for the "new thing" that God is doing cannot recognize it because it does not yet meet up to their unrealistically high standards.

The apostle Paul explained that the Lord calls the foolish of this world in order to confound the wise, and though He does not want us to remain foolish, it usually takes a while to rid ourselves of it! Just as Paul was emphatic, we must understand, the Lord does not want to appeal to the wise—*He wants to confound them!* **"God resists the proud and gives His grace to the humble" (James 4:6).** It takes humility to find the place of his grace, and the critical and idealistic will never look in the "stables" of this world to find that which is of God.

The Scriptures never described the ministry of heresy hunting. Even so, the Lord has used some of them to sound the alarm on such dangers as the New Age Movement, mostly because the elders of the church were not doing their job. However, the church does not need heresy hunters—she needs God-appointed elders with discernment who will sit in the gates of spiritual authority. Heresy hunters are usually self-appointed and often (not always) gain their influence by sowing paranoia in the church. The apostles and elders of the Biblical church did not gain their influence by exposing darkness, but by manifesting the light. Those who had the most light often did expose the darkness, but one who gains influence by only exposing darkness will have the wrong kind of influence in the church.

Skepticism has all of the appearance of wisdom, but it is the wisdom of the Tree of Knowledge of Good and Evil. Skepticism is not discernment and it powerfully undermines true faith. The apostolic exhortation in I Thessalonians 5:21 is to **"... examine everything carefully; hold fast to that which is good,"** (*not that which is bad*). If we read, or listen to preaching, while looking for what is wrong with it, we will not be able to see what is right.

So do we only read or listen to those who we know are absolutely right in everything? Of course not. The only One to ever walk the earth who was infallible is now in heaven. In almost every book and teaching that permeates the church there are some bones mixed in with the meat, and we just need to learn to pick out the bones. As the Lord put it, every time the Lord sows wheat in a field, the enemy comes along and sows tares "in the same field." The Lord could easily prevent this if He wanted to, but having us learn to deal with the tares is part of His curriculum. He did not even tell His workers to get the tares out—He said to "let them grow up together." It will not be until the field matures that we will really be able to tell the difference. If we try to sort out the tares prematurely, we will damage the wheat also, which is what happens in many revivals and spiritual movements.

## Emotions vs. the Will

Few would question that some of the emotional demonstrations still found in Pentecostal or Charismatic meetings are rooted in attention seeking, and sometimes they may even be demonic. But those who condemn such meetings because of the outbursts would have to also condemn the Lord's own meetings. When He walked the earth, there were the same kind of outbursts in His gatherings.

Contrary to some popular teachings, *love is an emotion.* The Lord Jesus actually encouraged emotional demonstrations of love for Him, such as the pouring out of the costly ointment and even the washing of His feet with tears.

What husband would want to hear from his wife that she no longer feels anything for him but serves him because it is her duty? What wife would care to be told by her husband that he loved her with the power of his will even though he had no feelings for her? Even though the marriage may still exist, the life is gone. Those who serve the Lord only by their will and not with their emotions have likewise lost the life in their union with the Lord. Do you think the Lord receives our hymns during worship if we are only singing out of duty and do not feel anything for Him? Just as the Lord exhorted through many of His prophets, such worship is vain. True worship can only be found in the proper balance between the will and the emotions, but we must have both.

When people have been subject to nothing but cold, lifeless religion and are suddenly touched by the living God, it is impossible for most not to become emotional, and they often go to the other extreme for awhile, becoming too emotional. It is of course best to be properly balanced, but if we must have an extreme, it would certainly be better to be extreme in our show of emotion for Him. Our Pharisaical nature will always be offended at this, just as they were in the Lord's meetings. Yet, when we become raging maniacs at our favorite sporting event, this only shows who we really worship.

It is impossible to feel God's presence without *feeling* a passionate love for Him. God created man to be both reasoning and emotional, and a redeemed man should be one who more than anyone maintains the proper balance between them. Spiritual maturity is doing the right things for the right reasons, with the right feelings. If man is deprived of either the ability to reason or to show his emotions, he has been deprived of half of his humanity.

Though it may be unintentional, those who attack emotional responses to the Lord are, in fact, stealing the life from our worship. Emotions are not meant to be the thermostat of human personality, but they are a relatively accurate thermometer. That is, our emotions should not control us, but they do reveal us.

# Chapter Sixteen

# Organization vs. Freedom

The organization (or lack of organization) of the Welsh Revival is an interesting study in itself. The leaders of this revival attained an uncommon level of sensitivity to the Holy Spirit that the whole church would do well to emulate. It is also probable that the Holy Spirit rested upon Wales in a greater measure, or in more intensity, than He has ever done either before or since. However, it was their strength in being so open to the Holy Spirit that the enemy used to push them too far, so that they actually prohibited the organization that was needed to help preserve the great advances that were made. Because of this, just a couple of years after the revival, evidence of it was scarce, and the whole nation quickly drifted back to its former depravity.

During the age of exploration a continual battle was waged between the explorers and the settlers. Neither liked or understood the other, but both were needed for the possessing of the new lands. The same is true spiritually. The spiritual pioneers usually do not like or understand the spiritual settlers, but both are needed for lasting spiritual advancement. If either group totally wins out over the other one, ultimate defeat is assured. If the settlers do not allow the exploration of new places, the corruption of stagnation will settle in. If the explorers do not tolerate the settlers, no one will ever benefit from all of the new places they find.

Many of the great revivals or awakenings in history were completely unplanned and remained in a state of perpetual disorganization, including the first century church for the first twenty or thirty years. Then it began to swing toward over-organization as the power and presence of the Lord was replaced by ritual and the newly formed traditions. There have been many missionary outreaches, such as the Salvation Army, that were highly effective in their time, and arguably have accomplished as much for the purposes of God over a period of time as was accomplished during the much more explosive Welsh Revival. Overall it seems improbable that the church has found the balance that allows organization to serve the purposes of the Holy Spirit without usurping His place.

True revivals are the high water marks of history. Anyone who has been touched by even the smallest revival, or spiritual awakening, seem destined to be forever spoiled for the presence of the Lord that is their hallmark. Even so, as Vance Havner so eloquently put it:

> Revival does not have all of the answers. Such resurgences can be compared to a sale in a department store. The sale may be more spectacular, but the main business is done in the daily merchandising the year round. Pentecost was a great day, but the steady growth came as the Lord added to the church daily. Revivals make headlines, but when the books are added up at the last day, it will be found that the main work was done by the faithful preaching of ordinary pastors, the daily witnessing of ordinary Christians, the soul-winning in home and church.

Let us continue to pray for revival, because it is certainly coming, but let us not neglect the important work of the kingdom that is in our hand to do today. Let us use every day to do the work that is before us and to prepare for the coming revival. In every great revival, awakening, or renewal of the church to date, much of the fruit was lost because the church was not prepared for it. Possibly for the first time in church history a great revival is now anticipated almost universally throughout the church. It is certainly probable that the reason the Lord has given us such a universal sense of impending revival is that we need this warning in order to be ready for it.

# Chapter Seventeen

# Unity Is Required

We know from the Scriptures that before the end of this age comes the church will be unified. The Lord is returning for a bride, not a harem! The prayers of Jesus will be answered and He prayed earnestly for the unity of His church.

When the Lord looks down upon the earth He sees only one church. The many divisions perpetrated upon the church were devised in hell, not heaven, and they will be overthrown before the end comes. We must have unity if we are going to be prepared for the great harvest that will mark the end of this age. The "nets" simply will not be able to hold the catch if we do not join together.

It is true that many are trying to unify the church for the wrong reasons and under the wrong spiritual organizations. Some, overreacting to this, decry all unity movements.

Others proclaim that only persecution can bring about the unity of the church. History testifies that this is not the case. During the terrible persecution of the church in Uganda under Idi Amin, the church in that country did come into a unity—all denominational barriers melted and the church seemed to truly be one. However, thirty days after the per-

**116**

secution was over, all of the previous barriers were erected again and the spiritual infighting picked up right where it left off before the persecution. This proved that the unity was only dictated by the external pressures and was not a true unity of the heart. Persecution can force us together for a time, but it does not correct the problems of the heart which cause the divisions.

It is by seeing the glory of the Lord that we will truly be changed and healed of the spiritual politics that so injure the Lord's body and our witness to the world. When the Lamb comes in, all of our crowns (personal positions) will be cast at His feet! Who can presume position or prestige in His presence? This was the unity that was brought about in the church in Wales during the revival. Only the Lord's presence can hold us together in true unity. But we must maintain His *presence* to maintain the unity.

## We Will Be Perfected In Unity

Only when the body is properly joined to the Head will all of the members function properly together. When the revival in Wales dissipated and the presence of the Lord lifted, the unity may have lasted a little longer than it did in Uganda, but eventually the church there also returned to its former divisions. But this is not true just of spiritual unity— the presence of the Lord is required for all true spiritual grace. We can only bear fruit as long as we *abide* (continue) in the Vine.

When the Lord prayed for the unity of the church, He prayed that we would be **"... perfected in unity, so that the world may know..."** that He was sent by the Father (see John 17:23). When the church comes into a true unity, not just a political agreement or compromise, then the whole world will know that Jesus is the Son of God.

When the Lord came down to see the tower that was being built in Babel, He stated: **'Behold, they are one people, and they all have the same language. And this is what they began to do, and now *nothing which they purpose to do will*** *be impossible for them"* (Genesis 11:6). For this reason the Lord scattered the languages of the men of Babel so that they could not continue building their vain tower. The Lord declared that **"... if two of you agree on earth about anything that they may ask, it shall be done for them by My Father who is in heaven"** (Matthew 18:19).

When just one hundred and twenty were in one accord on the Day of Pentecost the heavens opened and the church age was born. On that day a sign was given, the gift of tongues, by which all of the men who were present from so many different nations and languages, could understand what was being declared by God. These tongues were a sign that the church which was being born that day would be the anti-thesis of the tower of Babel. In the church men would again be unified and would be able to make it to heaven through Jesus, the One who would bring such unity.

## God Does Not Anoint Division

It is a basic Biblical and historic truth that God does not anoint division. No great revival or move of God has ever emerged from a divided church. The Lord pours out His Spirit only when there is a gathering "in one accord." The fundamental purpose of the kingdom of God is to restore unity and harmony in His divided creation. For the Lord to anoint anything less than unity is in conflict with His basic mission. The more unity the church has the more power it will receive. That is why Satan's fundamental strategy is to divide and turn believers against one another. Satan knows very well that one can put a thousand to flight but two can put ten thousand to flight—there is a multiplication of authority in unity.

The church will come into unity before the end, but there is a good reason why there has been so much disunity until now. There is a general, Biblical principle that between the place where we receive the promises of God, and the fulfillment of those promises (or Promised Land) there is usually a wilderness that is the exact opposite of what has been promised. An obvious example of this is Israel's exodus from Egypt, but we also see it in the life of almost every great Biblical character. We see this principle in the history of the church as well. She was promised to rule with the Lord over the nations, but for nearly two thousand years she has been ruled over by the world. She was meant to have a unity that would cause the whole world to believe in Jesus, yet she has probably been more divided than any other religion or philosophy.

Israel left Egypt in one day, but it took forty years in the wilderness to get the Egypt out of Israel and make them fit for the Promised Land. At one point when the Lord was about to destroy the whole nation and start again with Moses, he interceded, arguing that if the Lord destroyed Israel after bringing her out of Egypt, the whole world's testimony would be that the Lord could bring them out of Egypt but He could not bring them into their inheritance (see Exodus 32:1-14).

That is precisely the world's present testimony concerning the church—the Lord may be able to take us out of the world, but He has not been able to take the world out of us, or bring us into our spiritual inheritance. Before the end of this age the Lord will have a testimony through the church to the entire world that He was able to both take us out of our Egypt, and bring us into our inheritance. At the end of this age the Lord's prayer for unity will be answered and the whole world will know it—the result will be an outpouring of a power and authority that no one in the world will be able to deny.

# Chapter Eighteen

# The Control Spirit, Intolerance And Pharisaism

The control spirit, intolerance and spiritual Pharisaism are the most basic enemies of revival or renewal. It is one of the basic strategies of the enemy of our souls to enslave the church through "spiritual totalitarianism." This is done by controlling and oppressing believers through fear and intimidation. Fear is the counter-power to faith and the two are locked in a life and death struggle for every believer. One of the most important battlegrounds for the hearts of men is spiritual slavery versus spiritual liberty.

The apostle Paul stated, **"For with the heart man believes, resulting in righteousness..."** (Romans 10:10) Fear and intimidation can pressure men into believing with their minds, and even their emotions, but will never change men's hearts. Fear and intimidation used against someone will never result in their having a true faith. Fear is the power of the kingdom of darkness which enslaves. When fear is able to control us, then fear has, in one sense, become our lord.

The degree to which faith in God controls us determines His lordship in our lives. Faith is the power of the kingdom of God which sets men free to worship God in Spirit and truth. Fear rules men through external pressure and intimidation. Faith rules from the heart.

A parrot can be taught to say and do the right things, but they will not be in his heart—it is just "parroting." Acceptance which is based on intimidation or pressure will never result in true righteousness or a heart change, regardless of how accurate or true the doctrine is that is being forced upon us. To be true, our faith must come from the heart, not just the mind, because "living waters" can come only from the innermost being, the heart. We can never really live the truth unless we are able to live from our hearts. We will never be able to teach or preach that which imparts true life until we preach from our hearts where the true living waters abide. In order to be faithful to what is in the heart there must be freedom.

The tendency to associate the "heart" with feelings often causes confusion. Our feelings can come from our hearts, or they can come from other sources which are not our true heart. Few people, even few Christians really understand their own heart. Many have so covered their hearts with spiritual or social facades that they are not in touch with what is there. We also have the problem that Jeremiah described, **"The heart is more deceitful than all else and is desperately sick; who can understand it?** (Jeremiah 17:9). Even so, it is crucial that we do understand and live by a true heart because that is the only place from which genuine living waters can come.

One of the ultimate goals of true faith is to change men's hearts, then release them to live by their hearts. Because our hearts are the reservoir of the living waters, when we are freed to live by them, there is a release of the living waters for which all men are thirsting. Christians should be the most free and alive people on earth, and a striking contrast to the rest of humanity. When true, free Christians are seen they are unquestionably a great light on this earth. Unfortunately, there are not many free Christians.

Revival is essentially the release of the living waters within believers. This is why one of the greatest enemies of every revival has been the control spirit. The control spirit enslaves believers and stops the flow of living waters that creates and maintains every revival.

Satan obviously cares very little about what we believe as long as we believe in our minds and not with our hearts. In this way truth is used like an inoculation; we are given just enough to appease our consciences but not enough to change our hearts and bring forth a true faith and a release of living water. Satan's first strategy is to keep religion intellectual. He will give you as much truth as you want as long as he knows you will use it wrongly. When he sees the truths going beyond the intellectual realm and reaching hearts, he then sends a control spirit to stop it. Through a control spirit, Satan can use truths to bring men further into bondage. The Lord uses truth to set men free, but Satan can use truths to bring bondage when men submit themselves to a control spirit instead of the Holy Spirit.

## The Nature Of Obedience

The basic conflict between the kingdom of darkness and the kingdom of God concerns slavery and freedom. Jesus said: **"If you abide in My word, then you are truly disciples of Mine; and** *you shall know the truth, and the truth shall make you free"* (John 8:31-32). His truth will make us free as long as we abide in His word, but we must abide in His word. The truth makes us free and freedom is required to comprehend the truth from the heart. Obedience is important to the Lord, but God is not *just* after obedience—He wants us to obey for the right reasons, because we have His heart.

A women may wear a covering to church as a symbol of her submission to authority. Does wearing that covering make her submissive? Wearing the covering is not the submission, but is rather a symbol of it. A rebellious woman may also wear a covering; she may even do it as compensation for her rebellion and an attempt to disguise her lack of submission. The Lord does not ask us just to wear the symbols of our submission—He is looking for submission from the heart. Many of the doctrines promulgated by the church place more emphasis on the wearing of doctrinal "coverings" than on making the appropriate changes in our hearts.

If all that God required from man was obedience, He would not have given a choice to Adam and Eve in the garden. He could have easily programmed man to always obey, but then He would have had only robots. If there was going to be true obedience from the heart there also had to be the ability to disobey—there had to be freedom. That is why the Lord placed the Tree of the knowledge of Good and Evil in the garden; it was not placed there to cause man to stumble, but to be a point at which man could choose to obey Him. For there to be worship in spirit and truth, worship from the heart, then the ability to choose not to worship must also exist.

## Worship In Spirit

If God wanted only absolute obedience He could have created Adam and Eve so they could not disobey Him, but He did not even create the angels that way. What good is worship from one incapable of doing otherwise? If our typical "worship services" are an indication of the state of our worship, the Lord might have done just as well to program a thousand computers to sing praises to Him. If we are told when to stand, when to sit, what to sing, etc., we may have order, and it may sound good, but is it touching the heart of God? Typical church worship, whether it is traditional, Pentecostal, Charismatic, or Third Wave, is often little more than an attempt to warm up the audience for the main act—the preaching.

We must seek the Lord as to how to attain true worship in our services, because something must be done to rescue the church from these spiritual ruts. Unless worship enables our hearts to touch the heart of God it is not worship at all—it is just noise. If we touch the heart of God our hearts will be changed. Every worship service should be an encounter with the presence of the Lord. When we behold the glory of the Lord we will be changed by that glory. However, true worship does not come by *trying* to see the Lord, it comes from seeing Him.

There are some obvious, practical steps that could be taken to help bring a reality to our worship services. First, why not let the people sit if they want to? If the people have the freedom to sit, when they stand it will be to truly honor the Lord. The "singing in the spirit" that was born (or reborn) during the Welsh Revival can also be a wonderful format for allowing individuals to truly touch the heart of God with their own worship. It is true that when it is mechanical, or just another tradition, it is counterproductive, but when believers are released to sing what is in their own hearts to the Lord we have the greatest potential for entering worship that is in spirit and truth.

Most congregations do need worship leaders to give some order and direction to a service, and in this he may be the vessel of the Holy Spirit. But if we are going to touch true worship, there is a point when the worship leader must move out of the way, because as long as we have our attention on the leader we are not really worshipping the Lord from our own hearts, we are following a leader.

I have been in many congregations who did not have a worship leader because they claimed to be led entirely by the Holy Spirit, but were in fact being led more often by the immature and the rebellious. To release a congregation in this effort prematurely can be disastrous, but we should have a vision of maturing to that level. There is a point where true worship can bring such a manifest presence of the Lord that neither the flesh nor the devil will dare to show themselves.

But even if the flesh and the devil do get in from time to time, it may be better to have some occasional wild fires than to not have any fire at all. For there to be the potential for obedience from the heart, God had to give man a choice. The greater the freedom to choose, the greater the potential for choosing wrongly, and the greater the potential for true heart obedience to God. When we erect excessive controls, walls and barriers, around our services, programs or doctrines, so that they cannot be disobeyed, then we are only creating spiritual robots who may behave properly, but without true conviction from the heart. This is actually counterproductive to producing true Christian faith.

## His Sheep Know His Voice

As the apostle taught, **"Now the Lord is the Spirit, and where the Spirit of the Lord is there is liberty"** (II Corinthians 3:17). If we are going to walk by the Spirit there must be liberty. When we erect a system of rules and regulations to force obedience, we are prohibiting our ability to walk by the Spirit. The New Testament was not meant to be just another Law; it was meant to give us general guidelines while promoting the freedom for us to hear from the Lord ourselves about most issues, even very important ones. The Lord's sheep must know His voice and the freedom of the New Testament is meant to compel each of us to seek Him and to know Him for ourselves.

For example, the Lord does care very much about having His church built according to His own design, but the New Testament is surprisingly ambiguous about both church government and church structure, purposely. This is not so that we can just do whatever we want, but so that we must seek Him and hear from Him to get His instructions. There are some important general principles that we can find as a pattern in the New Testament about church structure, but they are meant to be general so as to promote the need for His builders to each seek Him and hear from Him, because He is the true Builder of the house.

The Lord gave us the New Testament to outline some clear general guidelines about life, the church, how we relate to governments, etc., that we must comply with to stay on the path of life. However, these guidelines are general enough to allow for and promote liberty. This is not liberty for the sake of license, but so that we would have to seek Him and follow the Holy Spirit in order to be led into "all" truth. The Lord did not say that when He went away He was going to leave us a book to lead us into all truth, but that He was going to give us His Holy Spirit to lead us into all truth. We should be very thankful for the priceless book that He left to us, but He never meant for it to take His place in our lives. When this happens it is being misused.

True Christianity is essentially a relationship with Christ, and relationship is essentially communication. As the Lord Jesus affirmed during His own temptation, **"Man shall not live by bread alone, but by every word that *proceeds* out of the mouth of God"** (Matthew 4:4, KJV). Note that this is the word that "proceeds," present tense, not that "proceeded," past tense. It is not enough for us to live by what He has said in the past, but we must be hearing from Him today. This is not to imply that this is for the establishing of new doctrines, or to add to the canon of Scripture, but that there is a living, personal relationship which we must all have with Him.

This was the lesson of the manna in the wilderness—it had to be gathered fresh everyday. We too must hear from Him everyday—we are called to live by a proceeding word, which reflects a continuing relationship. The quality of every relationship is based on communication. The quality of our faith is based on our communication with the Lord, and the New Testament was meant to promote the liberty that enables, and even requires, each one of us to develop that communication.

Freedom is a prerequisite for a true relationship. If a man forces relations with his wife he is committing rape, not love. The Lord, of course, would not rape His bride, the church, but he woos her, causing her to desire submission out of love. It is the evil one who forces and pressures us into obedience or commitments, and such will never bring forth true righteousness which can only come from the heart. Manipulation, intimidation and control are not from the Spirit of Truth, but are evil spirits that drive men from the truth and seek to bind them in darkness.

## The Modern Pharisees

One of the great spiritual battlegrounds of the Reformation was Satan's attempt to keep the Bible out of the hands of the common people. This battle continues to rage today because Satan knows very well that when the "common people" receive the word of God the revolution has begun, and he is about to be overthrown as the prince of this evil age. For this reason the Lord stated as evidence that He was indeed the Messiah that "the poor have the gospel preached to them." The Lord does love the poor, but this also has a strategic significance. Present rulers, even spiritual rulers, are usually too comfortable, and too protective of their territory, to respond to the word of God in radical obedience. Indeed, radical obedience is required to release the living waters from which revival springs. True revival is a revolution against the prevailing principalities and powers.

This battle to keep the word of God out of the hands of the common people was also raging in Israel when the Lord Himself walked the earth. Interestingly, the Pharisees, who loved and esteemed the Scriptures possibly more than any other sect of their time, were the enemy's main force of arms in this battle.

Because of their devotion to the scriptures, they were given the primary responsibility for maintaining the integrity of the Bible through centuries of copying and recopying. For this every lover of the Scriptures does owe them much. But in their zeal to protect the Scriptures from abuse, the Pharisees implemented a system of interpretation based more on their own tradition than on the actual text. These traditions caused them to miss, and even persecute, the One who was the personified Word of God—Jesus.

Today there are ultra conservative camps in Christianity in which modern Pharisees are doing essentially the same thing that their spiritual counterparts did. In their zeal to protect the Scriptures from doctrinal abuse they have erected a reactionary system of interpretation. This system does in fact protect the Scriptures from misinterpretation, but at the same time it works to hinder those who would radically obey the truth from receiving it.

Everyone who loves the truth wants to have accurate doctrine. However, when we stand before the judgment seat of Christ, we will not be judged on how accurate our doctrines were, but by our deeds. Accurate doctrine is not an end in itself, but a means to our being conformed to the image of Christ to better enable us to abide in Him. Sound doctrine enables us to better determine the will of God so that we can obey Him. But we can have the Bible memorized yet still not know the Truth because Truth is a Person. The Pharisees loved the Scriptures more than they loved the God of the Scriptures; we must be careful not to fall prey to this same deception. We cannot love God without loving His word, but we can elevate the written word above Him and make an idol out of the Scriptures, allowing them to supplant our relationship to Him, and to remove the Holy Spirit from the church.

Most believers are not in danger of esteeming the written word too much, but rather of esteeming it too little and neglecting this priceless gift from the Lord to His people. However, much of this neglect is caused by the ecclesiastical professionals who have imparted such a fear of error that many Christians are afraid to search for truth. At the same time many Christian leaders have esteemed the written word above the living Word and have begun to worship the book of the Lord in place of the Lord of the book. This has caused them to make the New Testament into just another law.

Just as the Pharisees, the greatest lovers of the Scriptures, were the greatest enemy of the Word Himself, some of those who are most outwardly devoted to protecting the integrity of the word are the greatest enemies of the truth today. These modern Pharisees work through fear and intimidation, the arch enemies of truth. Those who are controlled by fear will be the most threatened by anyone whom they cannot control through intimidation.

People who believe God with their hearts know the One in whom they believe. When we know that we are known by God, we will not be overly concerned about what anyone else thinks of us. Therefore we will not be threatened or intimidated by anyone on earth. Those with this constitution will make choices based on what is right, not out of political pressures that have such an appearance of righteousness but are in conflict with the Spirit of truth Himself.

## False Brethren

Jesus was tolerant of sinners but had little tolerance for the Pharisees and doctors of the law. These were not entering the kingdom and would not allow others to enter either. Modern Pharisees perceive those who have deviated from their interpretation of doctrines as enemies, false teachers, or false prophets. There are, of course, some false teachers and false prophets. However, the apostle Paul's description of false brethren is quite different from what is now popularly accepted. He warned against **"...false brethren who had sneaked in to *spy out our liberty* which we have in Christ Jesus, *in order to bring us into bondage"* (Galatians 2:4).** Those who use fear and intimidation to force others to conform to their beliefs should more often be categorized as false teachers than those they often so vehemently attack.

Liberty of the Spirit is essential in order to worship "in Spirit and truth." The same battle to infringe on the believer's spiritual liberty which raged in the early church is still raging today. If we are going to worship in Spirit and truth, we cannot compromise a believer's freedom to have differences in the nonessential doctrines and beliefs. Those who infringe upon this liberty are the greatest enemies of the truth, even if their stated intent is to protect the truth.

To declare that something is not Scriptural because it is not found in the Scriptures is a wrong application of the Scriptures. The Scriptures were given to free us to do whatever is not specifically banned, not to keep us from doing everything that is not mentioned in them. We must give believers the freedom to do what is not specifically banned in the New Testament, and then judge their fruit as to whether it was of God or not. This freedom does not mean that everything that we do is right; it simply means that in those matters we must seek the Lord individually for His will and also judgment.

There are times when the Lord would rather us use our own judgment than hear from Him about a matter. As we mature, He would rather us use our own judgment most of the time. If I tell my daughter to witness to one of her friends and she does it, it may please me to a degree, but not nearly as much as if she does it of her own accord. The first century apostolic teams were not led around by the hand; they were *sent* by God. They used their own judgment most of the time because they had His mind. When the Lord needed to give them special direction, or change their direction, He gave them a dream, vision, or prophetic word; but by the testimony of the Scriptures, that was in fact rare.

The Lord wants all of His people to know His voice and to have a personal and intimate relationship with Him. All relationships are based on communication, but not all communication is directive. Many people become addicted to prophetic words, which leads to a tragic misuse of the prophetic word. I must be very specific and give almost continual guidance to my two-year old, but much less with my eight-year old. As we mature, we should need less guidance, not more. Having to hear from the Lord about every little decision can be a sign of immaturity, not maturity.

Prophets are not meant to be gurus. Neither are the Scriptures meant to be used as a horoscope. Even so, for there to be the freedom for believers to know the Lord for themselves, to develop their own relationship to Him, and to know His voice, there must also be the freedom for them to make their own mistakes along the way.

Nothing is impossible with God. It would actually be a small thing for Him to have all Christians believing exactly alike about every doctrine. But true unity of heart will never be attained unless there is a choice not to be unified. Spiritual unity is not based on like doctrines; it is based on love—first for God and then for each other. By God's design we presently "see through a glass darkly." Each is able to see but a part of the whole picture, and we will never see the whole picture until we learn to put our parts together. God's unity is not a unity of conformity but a unity of many diverse parts. True heart faith is evidenced by tolerance for those who are different, which is required if there is going to be a true unity of the heart.

## Each Must Gather His Own Manna

When the children of Israel were given manna from heaven, each household had to gather its own. The same holds true for gathering heavenly manna. We cannot rely solely upon the leaders for our spiritual food. This is not to belittle the importance of leaders and teachers who give themselves to the word and the ministry. Just as the Levites were essential for ministering to the congregation of Israel, our leaders are essential today. But leaders cannot take on the duty of the individual or the individual household. There is a difference between the general teaching that should be provided by those devoted to the ministry of the word, and the daily bread from heaven which must be gathered by each household.

How can an untrained person go to the Bible for a fresh word from heaven without falling into error or false teaching? This is one of the most important issues which has faced God's people during the four thousand years since the written word was first given to man. One of Christianity's greatest struggles has been for the freedom of ordinary people to have access to and interpret the Scriptures for themselves. Even those movements most devoted to Restoration or Renewal have almost all eventually developed a tight doctrinal statement that prohibits departure from "the party line." Then they usually develop systems and methods of interpreting the Scriptures (hermeneutics) which tend to take this ability out of the hands of the people and keep Biblical interpretation solely in the hands of the leaders. Often this can help restrict the misinterpretation and misuse of Scripture, but the very barriers that we erect to protect the Scriptures prohibit further spiritual progress or growth.

## Hermeneutical Problems

Most of the hermeneutical systems that have been developed for the noble purpose of trying to prevent heresy or errors also destroy the liberty that is required for a believer to develop his own relationship with the Lord and to worship Him in Spirit and truth. Unfortunately, many of the remedies have too often proven more harmful than the diseases they were designed to treat. This is not a statement against the proper development and use of hermeneutics. (Hermeneutics is simply a system of interpretation). This is a statement against choking the ability of individuals to read and understand the Scriptures for themselves.

Both Catholic and Conservative Protestant hermeneutics have been guilty of doing this. Like the Pharisees who preceded them, some of the most conservative denominational leaders have erected barriers to the ability of individuals to receive a fresh revelation or interpretation from the Scriptures. In fact the very word "fresh revelation" is usually cursed by them with the accusations of men seeking to add to the Scriptures, when this is not what is meant at all. The fresh revelation that is needed is an increased or deeper understanding of the Scriptures. Those who react so strongly to fresh revelation from the Scriptures have erred with one of the most terrible presumptions of all—the belief that they already know all that there is to know.

There are some outstanding hermeneutical principles that can help any sincere seeker of truth to stay on the path that leads to life. Unfortunately, these are often surrounded by many other principles that are designed to protect predetermined interpretations about many non-essential doctrines that are used to limit one's scope, vision, and understanding about Biblical teachings. There is obviously much more to be understood from the Bible than we now understand. Many aspects of conservative hermeneutics prevent, or at least greatly discourage, further exploration and understanding from the Scriptures.

With all its different theological camps, the church has become like the proverbial blind men and the elephant. The one who found the leg was sure the elephant was like a tree. The one who found the tail thought that was ridiculous; the elephant was like a rope! The one who found its ear thought that the other two were both mistaken; the thing was like a great leaf. They were all partially right but totally wrong. They could never identify the elephant until they listened to each other and combined their understanding.

The wise psalmist declared, **"The SUM of Thy word is truth" (Psalm 119:160).** Each of us may have a part that is true but it is not the whole *truth* until it is properly fitted together with the other parts of the body of Christ. Understanding and interchanging with the different camps of Biblical interpretation can help us to receive the good without stumbling over the bad. Those who know the Spirit of Truth will have the confidence in Him to do this. Unfortunately, those who are the most bound by fear, who need the interchange the most, will seldom have the confidence in the Holy Spirit to do this. Those who are bound by a control spirit will have more faith in the devil to deceive them than they will have in the Holy Spirit to lead them into all truth.

*There is a God ordained ambiguity preventing the establishment of an absolute law or method of Biblical interpretation. This ambiguity is designed to keep us dependent on the Holy Spirit to lead us to truth.* That men would presume that they could develop a system, or principles, by which they can interpret the Scriptures is in itself an act of profound human arrogance. Such principles try to lay the burden of interpretation on a science in place of the Holy Spirit, which is itself a departure from the nature of true Christianity—a relationship with God. If such a thing were possible, why are they not clearly laid out in the Scriptures, and why do the writers of Scripture themselves so often depart from these principles? As stated, there are some principles that can help us in our quest for Biblical truth; but there are no *absolute laws or methods* of Biblical interpretation. When we presume to substitute our own science for the Holy Spirit, we have by that fallen into serious error.

The Scriptures contain many paradoxes because the truth is found in the tension between the extremes. Only the Holy Spirit can enable us to discern such truth and keep us in the proper balance between the extremes that will cause us to depart from the course. Does this not open the doors for a great deal of subjectivity in interpreting the Scriptures? Yes! And that is the point. True Christianity promotes an extraordinary liberty for the personal quest of God's truth, a liberty that is required if we are going to believe from our hearts and not just our minds.

# Chapter Nineteen

# The Highest Form Of Unity

When we try to project increasingly absolute laws of interpretation, or doctrines, it may present a semblance of order and unity, but both the order and the unity will be external, not internal. As soon as the restraints are removed and we quickly see how much true order and unity there is; most of the time we will find chaos. As Martin Luther once quipped, "A spiritual man does not need a covenant (contract), and an unspiritual man cannot keep one!"

When we try to get men to comply with our doctrines or commit themselves to our fellowship with human covenants and commitments, we have probably nullified their ability to come into a true unity or a true faith in the doctrine. We have also probably set ourselves up for a future church split.

It is true that we are living in a day of increasing lawlessness. Truth, honor, and the belief that a man's word is his bond is becoming very hard to find. Even so, legalism is not the answer to lawlessness; it only feeds lawlessness, which is why Paul said, **"....the power of sin is the law"** and **"...the**

**letter kills, but the Spirit gives life"** (I Corinthians 15:56 & II Corinthians 3:6). When we apply the law to a person, we are only exacerbating the problem by highlighting it without giving the person the grace to overcome it—in this way we make sin manifest. If our constraints are strong enough, we may keep the person under control; but as soon as the restraints are removed he will be even worse. Using the law, we can lock up the criminal; but we cannot change him. As soon as he is released from our prison, he will continue to break the law because he has not been inwardly changed.

The Lord is seeking truth in the inner man. When we are true in our hearts, we will be true when no one is looking and when no one could find out because it is in our hearts. When we seek unity by putting external restraints on believers such as covenants and commitments that go beyond the New Covenant that we already have, we are trying to join men to ourselves instead of to Christ; and it will almost always end in a spiritual tragedy. Men may want to make the covenant when they make it, but all of us are going through the process of change; and when we try to hold men to us beyond the time when they want to remain, they may stay longer because of their commitment, but they will ultimately leave. When they do it will leave more destruction in the relationship, and probably more people will be affected by it, because of the guilt and bondage that has been imposed.

The Lord made it easy for His disciples to leave Him and difficult for them to stay. Why would we try to do it differently? Why would we want anyone committed to us if it is not in his heart? Only when a person is free to go, but he continues to stay, do we know that he is really with us in his heart.

To make a covenant is a serious matter, and breaking one can bring us under condemnation. The New Covenant which we have in Christ and the marriage covenant are the only covenants that are Biblical. If we are joined to Christ, we are already joined to His body, the church. When we are compelled to make covenants with people, local congregations, or movements, it is a covenant that is outside of the New Testament; and both the New Testament and history testifies that it will likely end badly. When Peter made the commitment that he would never deny the Lord, he could not even keep it through the night.

I have heard some very eloquent and moving messages about the beauty of David and Jonathan's covenant, but the tragic ending to that relationship is a poignant example— Jonathan still died in the house of Saul although he had committed himself to the house of David. However, one must also appreciate David's heart to keep the covenant even with Jonathan's children. A noble soul will keep his agreements even when the other party does not.

Why should we put people under unnecessary pressure to be joined to us or our work? This only reflects the shallowness of our leadership and the lack of the Lord's presence. When the Lord Jesus is lifted up, all men are going to be drawn to Him; and we do not need any other props. When we try to lift up ourselves or our works in His place, which is what we are doing when we pressure men to commit to us or to our work, they will inevitably become disappointed and be scattered, with great injury to all.

The first council in Jerusalem resulted in the most important declarations in church history, and they established a Biblical liberty for all Christians. After contending with the believers from the sect of the Pharisees, who had been compelling the young church to continue keeping the Law of Moses, the apostles and elders stated,

> **For it seemed good to the Holy Spirit and to us to lay upon you no greater burden than these essentials:**
>
> **That you abstain from things sacrificed to idols and from blood and from things strangled and from fornication; if you keep yourselves free from such things, you will do well. Farewell (Acts 15:28-29)**

Does this mean that we can do anything else, watch anything we want on television, look at pornography, gamble, etc.? Of course not. It means that we are all required to be led by the Holy Spirit and to obey Him. It means that we learn to walk by the "perfect law of love," and if we love the Lord, our families, the church, and our neighbors, we would not behave in ways that could hurt them.

The control spirit, which is often manifested through human covenants or the use of guilt and pressure, is the manifestation of counterfeit spiritual authority. We only have true spiritual authority to the degree that Jesus lives within us. When He lives within us, we are acutely aware that He is building His church, and that He is quite able to do it perfectly. Therefore, we can relax. When we minister in true spiritual authority we are yoked with Him, which means He is going to be the one pulling the weight—His yoke really is easy and His burden is light. When we take it, we really do find rest for our souls—we no longer have to strive.

Liberty is essential for a true Christian walk. Increasing liberty should always be our goal, but it must be understood that increasing liberty comes with increasing maturity. I cannot give my toddler nearly the liberty that I give her older sisters, or that I will give them when they become eighteen. Likewise, new believers generally need much more supervision and help than those who have been Christians longer. The real issue is: are we promoting spiritual liberty and truth that will change men's hearts, that is not based on human constraints and pressures, to get them to conform? We will never have true worship from the heart if we do not have this reality.

## Summary

There is substantial evidence that the enemy's most effective weapon in stopping revivals and true spiritual advancement has been the control spirit. He often uses the control spirit together with a political spirit, which attempts to cause leaders to care more about what men think that what God thinks. As the Lord warned the Pharisees: **"You are those** who justify yourselves in the sight of men, but God knows your hearts; for that which is highly esteemed among men is detestable in the sight of God" (Luke 16:15). If we are compelled to do that which is highly esteemed in the sight of men we will be doing what is detestable in the sight of God.

As Paul stated it: **"But a natural man does not accept the things of the Spirit of God; for they are foolishness to him..." (I Corinthians 2:14).** So that which is highly esteemed with men is detestable to God, and that which is of the Spirit of God is foolishness to men. Obviously we have a choice to make: we can please God or men, but we cannot please both. As Paul explained to the Galatians: **"If I were still trying to please men, I would not be a bond-servant of Christ" (Galatians 1:10).** Both the control spirit and the political spirit usually  gain their influence through the fear of man. If we are going to have a part in bringing true revival, we must be delivered from this fear and remain utterly focused on obeying the will of God.

# PART III

# The Coming Harvest

Chapter Twenty

# God Will Do It Again

As extraordinary as the Welsh Revival was, it was only a foretaste of the harvest that is the end of the age. Like the Israelite spies who brought back fruit from the promised land to testify of its abundance, the Welsh Revival was a foretaste of the abundance of God that is about to be realized as the church crosses its Jordan River to begin the conquest of her inheritance.

Just as the spies brought back several kinds of fruit (grapes, pomegranates and figs), the Welsh Revival was but one kind of the fruit we will find in our promised land. There may not have been another move of God in history that accomplished more in such a short period of time as the Welsh Revival, but the Great Awakenings that were ignited by the ministries of Jonathan Edwards, George Whitfield and the Wesleys were every bit as effective in turning multitudes to Christ, and had even more far reaching and longer lasting results. However, each of these awakenings and revivals were different. The Reformation movements that originated in Germany and Switzerland were extraordinary moves of God in their time, as were the Anabaptist, Pietist, Puritan and many other great movements. Each of them has contributed to the fabric that now makes up the living, advancing church.

There were doctrinal and practical differences between all of these great movements and revivals, but God used all of them. There is much common ground between them, but they all seemed to include an aspect of God's ways that the others lacked. Likewise they all seemed to include characteristics that were not God's ways or His truth, but He used them anyway.

Every revival, or renewal, in history has been at least a little bit out of control. However, it was this area that was beyond man's control that seemed to be the place where the Lord would move in the greatest way, but also where the devil or carnality would gain influence. Every field where the Lord sows wheat the enemy will come along and sow tares, but if we become so afraid of the tares that we will not go to that field we will not get the wheat either! This all seems by God's design to separate the cowards and unbelieving, both of whom He has declared will not enter His kingdom (see Revelation 21:8).

The Lord has had a few "Joshuas and Calebs" who have been outstanding in their time, full of faith and doing great exploits. Now, at the end of the age, He is raising up a generation who will follow the "Joshuas and Calebs" with the faith to cross over and possess their inheritance. Evan Roberts was a great man of faith and was used mightily, but the Lord is about to release ten thousand like him, along with others who will be more like William Booth, Hudson Taylor, John Wesley, George Whitfield, Jonathan Edwards, Count Zinzendorf, John Knox, Luther, Peter and even like Paul—*all at the same time!* There are many different kinds of fruit in the Promised Land. Together they will ignite a multitude of Welsh Revivals, multitudes of Great Awakenings and many Reformations—*together*.

We have come to the times that even the angels desired to see. There is a generation coming that will see all of the things that every prophet and righteous man from the beginning longed to see. For those who love God there has never been a greater day to be alive. The Lord really has saved His best wine for last.

## Prepare Or Perish

The eternal record will almost certainly establish that the Welsh Revival, like many other revivals in history, will pay a dear price in lost fruit because of church leadership's failure to heed the mandate of Ephesians Four—that the ministry of the church is given to equip the members who are to do the work of the service.

The last few years have brought to the church a world-wide expectation of revival and harvest. This has been exciting and encouraging, but we must understand that it is also a warning! There is much to do to get ready for this harvest, and precious little has been done so far. True revival is one of the great blessings that we can experience on this earth, but it can also be one of the great tragedies if we are not prepared for it. It is a fact that the churches that experience revival without being prepared for it are likely to be destroyed by it. If our nets are not strong enough to hold the catch they will break!

Certainly to have just experienced something like the Welsh Revival would be the memory of a lifetime, but we are called to much more than just making memories, we are called to bear fruit that *remains*. As powerful as the Welsh Revival was in its time, just a few years later a visitor to Wales could hardly tell that it had ever occurred. In studying this revival we have looked at an extraordinary piece of church history, but one that is relevant to both our present and our future. This is for the purpose of preparing and equipping the church to fulfill her great mandate for this hour and to bear fruit that remains.

The following is a brief account of a vision that I was given over a three day period in September of 1987. Some aspects of the vision are already history, the rest will soon be upon us. I have included it here just as it was written and distributed in 1987.

# Chapter Twenty-One

# A Vision Of The Harvest

To properly understand this vision you must keep in mind that it represents a GRADUAL unfolding which takes place over a period of time, possibly many years. Though I do not know the timing of these events, it is obvious that some are already beginning to take place. I do not know whether the complete unfolding takes five years or fifty. I do know that they will come as travail does upon a woman in labor. That is, they will come in waves with relative calm in between. As we get closer to the birth these "contractions" will become both more frequent and more intense until they are constant. I also perceive that the timing of these events will not be the same for all parts of the body of Christ.

Please let me include a caution. Much of this vision seems spectacular; its fulfillment will be even more so. Some who are foreseeing these things have begun to question works they are presently involved in as being irrelevant and destined to pass away. I think there are many works that should be questioned in this manner with or without the vision, but I know that many works which are destined to pass away in this coming move are presently serving the purpose of God and helping to prepare His way. I would question any drastic changes in direction caused by any vision.

**147**

This vision was given merely to aid and give confidence in the preparation He is already working in His people. Do with all of your heart what He has given you to do. If we are abiding in Him, the changes that are coming will be an exhilarating fulfillment of His work, not its destruction. When the Lord fulfilled the Law it did pass away, but it did so with glory. When Jesus fulfilled it, for the first time its true purpose and all that it had accomplished was realized.

Many works will fade in this coming move, but they too will do so with great glory if they are indeed His work. Only do not be like many in Israel who worshipped the Law more than what it was meant to prepare them for—Jesus. All true ministry is for the same purpose—to prepare us for Him. Like the Law, when He appears, the ministry may no longer be needed. If He is the one we are seeking and serving, that will not matter—He will be our fulfillment.

In this vision I do not see beyond the harvest. I believe I understand somewhat the unfolding plan of God beyond this but that is my interpretation of the Scriptures. As it was not given as a part of this vision I do not feel that it should be included here. I believe the Scriptures verify this vision but I have included few here to leave room for the Lord to speak individually to those who receive it.

## Part I

The Lord has revealed to many that there will soon be a great outpouring of His Spirit. This revival will be greater than all those preceding it. This vision includes key elements to this coming harvest and what the Lord is doing in the church now to prepare for it.

This outpouring will ultimately result in some very radical changes for both the church and the world. These need to be understood by those who would be used by God for one of the greatest events in history. To those who are diligent seekers of God and obedient to His will, this vision does not represent disruption. These things will happen to them as a natural flow of the Spirit moving them to increased light and intimacy with Him. Those that are comfortable and resist change will have a very hard time. I ask you to openly and prayerfully reflect on what I am herein sharing with you. Some of these things may not speak to you now, but I believe they will in the future and will give you great peace and confidence as you remember them.

For the coming harvest the Lord is preparing a great spiritual "fishnet", one able to hold the catch that is coming. This net is formed by the linking together of His people. The links in this net are the interrelationships of His people. The stronger the intercommunication and interrelationships, the stronger this net will be. It is not only happening in the local churches among members, but between ministries and congregations throughout cities, states, and crossing international barriers around the world.

In Ephesians 4:15-16, we see this principle: "**... we are to grow up in all aspects into Him, who is the Head, even Christ, from whom the whole body, being fitted and held together by that which every JOINT supplies....**" A joint is not a part, but it is where two or more parts come together. There is a great fitting together going on in the Spirit now and it will increase in the near future, on all levels.

The Spirit is compelling pastors to get together with other pastors, prophets with prophets, apostles with apostles, and even whole congregations are beginning to visit and interrelate with other congregations apart from their own circles of emphasis. This is the Lord's doing. Some of these meetings may seem fruitless because of improper agendas but they will bear fruit, there will be links made. Soon the Lord's presence in these meetings will melt all presumption and the facades which separate us from union with Him and each other. His presence will stimulate a worship that brings about Psalm 133 unity—as we anoint the Head with our worship the oil will flow down to the edge of His robes— covering the entire body.

He is beginning this breakdown of barriers with the leadership because this is where most originate and where they are the strongest. As the walls come down here the entire body will begin to flow together. If the leaders resist this move the Lord will continue through the congregations. These will begin to relate to other members of the body of Christ and their bonds will grow stronger regardless of the resistance or warnings of their pastors. Some pastors and leaders who continue to resist this tide of unity will be removed from their place. Some will become so hardened they will become opposers and resist God to the end. Most will be changed and repent of their resistance.

Because of the magnitude of the "catch" this net will be rent many times and will be in need of constant mending. The Lord will use much of the discord now taking place in the church to prepare those whose task in the harvest will be almost exclusively devoted to the mending and binding of this great net. These peacemakers will have a great part in building this net and a major impact on the effectiveness of the entire revival. Those that seem to always find themselves in the middle of conflicts should be encouraged with the knowledge that they are being prepared for a great work.

Some that were used greatly of God in the past have become too rigid in doctrinal emphasis, or are too entangled with spiritual "Ishmaels", to participate in this revival. Some of these will try to join the work but their interrelationships will be so superficial that they will quickly be torn from the net with the first catch. Those who are linked together by doctrine or who gather around personalities will quickly be torn away. Only those who are joined by and through Jesus alone will stand the pressure this harvest will bring upon the church (Colossians 1:17).

The redemption of so many will bring much joy but they will come with problems, bringing enormous stress to congregations and ministers. The cords of unity must be very strong to withstand this pressure. Those who have not yet learned to take the Lord's yoke will be overwhelmed while trying to carry the burdens themselves. Entering the Sabbath rest of the Lord will become a major emphasis in preparation for the harvest. Heed this word!

A large number who are now considered Christians, even "spirit-baptized" Christians, have never been led to the Lord. They were led to the church, to a personality, or to a doctrine or emphasis. Some of these will think they are important links in the net but will actually become part of the harvest, starting over again on the proper Foundation—Jesus. This group includes many well known ministers and pastors. Their humility in this will lead multitudes to question and strengthen their own relationships to the Lord. This will strengthen and encourage the entire body of Christ.

Many denominations, extra-local fellowships and circles of emphasis will begin disbanding and severing those ties, even those that were ordained by God for a season, in order to take their place in this great net that the Lord is now forming. For some these ties will just be ignored or forgotten until they have passed away, almost without notice, because of the greater intensity and substance of this new move. For others it will be a very painful rending as they are persecuted and rejected by those who do not understand. Those who are required to leave much behind will soon receive many times that which they have left.

Some leaders will actually disband their organizations when they realize they are no longer relevant to what God is doing. Others will just leave them behind to disband of themselves. In becoming part of this harvest, all circles of ministry or influence with individual identities will ultimately dissolve into a single identity of simply being Christians. Single presbyteries will form over cities and localities. These will be made up of pastors and leaders from all different backgrounds. Their unity and harmony in purpose, as well as that of the various congregations, will become a marvel to the world. The Lord will give these presbyteries great wisdom and discernment but there will be no doubt that Jesus alone will be the Head of His church. What is coming will be bigger than any man or council of men could control or administrate.

The Lord's purpose in preparing for the harvest is to JOIN, not to separate. The dismantling of organizations and disbanding of some works will be a positive and exhilarating experience for the Lord's faithful servants. They will not be just leaving something behind, they will be going on to a much greater work. Those who have fallen to worship the work of God more than the God of the work will have trouble, but most of these too will be set free by the tremendous anointing that is coming. Those that feel called to attack and tear down the old will not be sent from the Lord. There will be many "stumbling blocks" circulating in the church that will cause confusion and some destruction from time to time. They will perceive themselves as prophets sent to judge and deliver. Those serving in leadership must trust their discernment and REMOVE the stumbling blocks.

To be distinguished from the "stumbling blocks," the Lord will raise up a great company of prophets, teachers, pastors and apostles that will be of the spirit of Phinehas. Just as the son of Eleazar could not tolerate iniquity in the camp of the Lord, this "ministry of Phinehas" will save congregations, and at times, even whole nations, from the plagues that will be sweeping the earth. They will be moved by the jealousy of the Lord for the purity of His people. They will be sent to save and preserve the work of the Lord, not to tear down as the stumbling blocks so fashion themselves.

## Part II

For a time, there will be such an inflow of people that even this great net will not be able to hold them all. Many of the former works and organized churches will be swelled with this overflow. Because of this they will assert that they are both the cause and primary purpose for this revival. This delusion will not last long because concurrent with the harvest there will be gripping tribulation in the world which will eventually consume them. This is the judgment of the Lord against the works He did not commission: The great "sea," or mass of humanity, that they sought to rule, will rise up to destroy them.

Wars will increase. There will even be some nuclear exchanges but on a limited basis, mostly between third world nations. Far more will perish by plagues and natural disasters than by wars during the period of this vision. The very foundations of civilization will shake and erode. Even the world's most stable governments will be melting like wax, losing authority and control over their populations.Eventually it will be hard to find anyone with the courage to assume authority. This will cause sweeping paranoia throughout the entire earth.

Huge mobs will attack everything in their path. The infrastructure of the great denominational churches and large visible ministries will be one of their primary targets and will vanish almost overnight. Pagan religions, cults and witchcraft will spread like plagues but these will also become targets of the mobs. By this time governments will have broken down to the point where lynching and mass executions perpetrated by these mobs are overlooked by the authorities. Fear and deep darkness will cover the earth, but this will just make the glory which is appearing upon the saints more striking. Huge masses of people will be streaming to the Lord, the inflow so great in places that very young Christians will be pastoring large bodies of believers. Arenas and stadiums will overflow nightly as the believers come together to hear the apostles and teachers.

At this time few congregations will remain separate or individual entities. Many elders and pastors may be stationary but groups they oversee will be constantly changing. Some of these will be moving on because of persecution and others because the Lord will scatter them to carry His message abroad like seed. Near the end (of the vision) the body of Christ has become like a great flowing river sweeping about as freely as the wind. One day there may be meetings in a public auditorium or stadium, the next day in a park, and continually from house to house. Great meetings that stir entire cities will happen spontaneously. Extraordinary miracles will be common while those considered great today will be performed almost without notice by young believers.

Angelic appearances will be common to the saints and a visible glory of the Lord will appear upon some for extended periods of time as power flows through them.

Conferences of apostles, prophets, pastors, elders, etc.. will be called and used greatly by the Lord, but without denominating and separating from the rest of the body. Their unity will be in Jesus and He alone will be the Head of His church. Eventually, The Lord's presence will be so great during this revival that, like the twenty-four elders in Revelation, all crowns will be cast at His feet and spiritual presumption will be unthinkable.

Those in leadership will be the most humble of all. Those who presume leadership without calling will be apparent to all. The leaders of this move will be true servants, not interested in reputation or position. Their humility will open them to become channels for wave after wave of living water. **"He will dwell with the humble of the land."**

This harvest will be so great that no one will look back at the early church as a standard; all will be saying that the Lord has certainly saved His best wine for last. The early church was a firstfruits offering, truly this will be a harvest! It was said of the Apostle Paul that he was turning the world upside down; it will be said of the apostles soon to be anointed that they have turned an upside down world right side up. Nations will tremble at the mention of their name.

These men and women of God will take little notice of their own accomplishments because of their burning love for the One who works through them and the recognition of His accomplishments. Like Jesus, they will flee to the mountains when men try to make them kings or exalt them in any way. Their exaltation or authority will not come through man, it will only come from above. As the masses will be seeking anyone to take authority during these times, this comes as a warning! If the people make a man king, who rules? The authority established by the Lord will be very different than what even His own people now perceive. Do not try to rule, just SERVE. Through this His authority will flow and begin to bring order though Peace.

## Part III

I do not believe the actual magnitude of these events can be expressed here, neither the chaos nor the move of the Holy Spirit. As to the "rapture" or second appearance of the Lord Jesus, I have my own ideas but was not given anything concerning them in this vision. What I was allowed to foresee ended with increasing chaos and increasing revival.

There will be words and exhortations, originating from the very throne of the Lord and carrying great authority, coming to prepare His church for the days to come. Among the numberous exhortations coming, we will soon hear His preachers, prophets and teachers begin to emphasize the following:

1. BUILD UPON THE ONLY FOUNDATION THAT CAN BE LAID. JESUS HIMSELF. Works that are built upon truths instead of The Truth will not stand in this day. Many of today's congregations and ministries are devastated by the slightest shaking. The works that are properly built on Jesus will withstand the greatest trials and attacks without being moved. There will be a great emphasis on the Lord Jesus Himself in the days to come. The increasing revelation of Him will overshadow the many emphases of the past like the sun does the moon when it rises. The truths that have been such a distraction will begin to seem insignificant as the church begins to see Him **"in whom are hidden ALL of the treasures of wisdom and knowledge"** (Colossians 2:3).

2. REMOVE THE BARRIERS AND FACADES THAT SEPARATE US FROM THE LORD AND EACH OTHER. We must become more intimate with Him, and through Him, each other. Spiritual pride and the exaltation of men, individual truths, or works, will come under unrelenting discipline from the Lord and will soon be understood as "strange fire". Those who continue to offer it will perish from the ministry with such demonstration that a pure and holy fear

of the Lord will sweep through the body of Christ. This will help the church to move into true spiritual worship and a unity that is based on that worship.

3. ABIDE IN THE SABBATH REST OF THE LORD. This will become an increasing emphasis in the teaching and a reality as the Lord enters His temple, the church. Our growing intimacy with Him will bring a peace that will actually calm the storm of the rising sea of humanity. The intensity of the times will overwhelm any pseudo peace. We must be one with the "Lord of the Sabbath."

4. HEED THE SPIRITUAL PREPARATION WHICH MAY BE REFLECTED IN THE NATURAL. For example: Some have begun moving their assets into precious metals or land. This may be helpful, but it is far more important to take the spiritual land and to lay up our treasures in heaven. The Lord is seeking givers who will become channels of His supply. For them there will be no lack. Those that hoard or do not learn to freely give may suffer increasing crisis in their earthly affairs. This is the Lord's discipline to set them free. Some who are faithful and generous givers may also experience increasing crisis in this, but it is for their preparation to become great channels for the provision of many. Remember Joseph!

Some are feeling they should limit their travel to certain areas and are beginning to emphasize cleanliness because of the AIDS epidemic. This may be helpful, but there is only one deliverance from the judgments of God—to be found in Christ. Spiritual purity is far more important than the natural and can alone protect us from AIDS or any other plague.

5. "THE JUST SHALL LIVE BY FAITH," NOT FEAR. Fear will greatly increase in the world. Actions taken by the church because of fear will almost always prove destructive. Some "faith teaching" has muddied the waters to the degree that some do not even want to hear the word "faith." This frequently happens before the Lord begins a great work. A great revelation of true faith is coming; it will be an essential revelation for us to serve in these days. Some will be called

to walk where angels fear to tread. KNOW that He who is in us is MUCH greater than he who is in the world. The vessels He is now preparing will walk in a boldness and confidence that will astonish a world gripped in fear. Our faith will grow as the presence of the Lord increases. True faith is the recognition of the One in whom we believe. When we truly and properly fear the Lord we will not fear anything else.

In the coming days many will exist in the miraculous on a continual basis. This will become as natural to them as the gathering of manna was to Israel. Some of the Lord's exploits on behalf of His people will be UNPRECEDENTED, exceeding the greatest Biblical miracles. These will seem almost normal and will take place because the presence of the Lord will cause more wonderment than His works. He will be very close to His people in these days.

6. THE LORD WILL SOON OPEN OUR UNDERSTANDING OF HIS WORD AND PURPOSES TO A DEPTH BEYOND OUR PRESENT COMPREHENSION. The "books" are yet to be "opened" as they will be. When they are, our understanding of even basic truths, such as salvation, being born again, etc., will be enormously increased. This will give far more substance and depth of purpose to the entire body of Christ. The functions of the gifts and ministries will come with increasing authority and power as our confidence increases with knowledge. The spiritual dimension will become more real to the church than the natural. When the proper Foundation has been adequately laid in the church (our union and devotion to Jesus Himself), the Spirit of Revelation will be poured out as never before.

## Part IV

The Charismatic and Third Wave renewals were notable moves of the Holy Spirit. Though the fruit at times may have seemed to be superficial, multitudes did meet the Lord. The tragedy has been that so many were lost again to the world. Even so, much was accomplished and many of those brought into the kingdom remained and matured. He now has what will prove to be a strong foundation to build upon, a net to hold the catch that He has prepared for the end of the age. Through the tribulations and dry times of the last few years He has been carefully weaving strong cords which He is now beginning to bind together.

Do not resist the Lord in this work. Seek greater intimacy with the Lord and open yourself to your fellow members in the body of Christ. Reach out to them and  remove the barriers. Those who have drifted into extremes will be brought back to the course never again to be distracted from the River of Life by the little tributaries that feed it. Those who have resisted new truth will soon be diving into the River, fearless of rocks or depths. The anointing will soon break all of our yokes. The Reformation showed us the Way. The Pentecostal and Charismatic renewals began leading us on to Truth. Through the revival that is coming we will come to know Jesus as our Life. When the cord has all three strands it will not be easily broken.

This word is given for the PREPARATION of those the Lord desires to use. Relationships are about to be built between ministries and congregations that have feared and rejected each other in the past. He will do this in many without changing their doctrines or emphasis; He will merely cause His people to rise above such differences and worship Him in unity. As He is lifted up we will gradually begin to wonder how many things that were so important to us, and often divided us, could have had so much of our attention. As this final battle begins we are all going to be amazed, and sometimes ashamed, at those we find on our side.

We must humble ourselves under His mighty hand so that we may take part in a great exaltation. Those who allow themselves to be emptied, who lay aside all personal ambition to become of no reputation, who patiently suffer rejection and misunderstanding, will soon stir the entire world with the King's message.